ACHIEVING
the Balance

3 SIMPLE RULES
AND
3 BASIC TOOLS

ACHIEVING
the Balance

Leo Weidner
Mark Kastleman

LifeBalance Institute, LLC

LifeBalance Institute and its logo are trademarks of
LifeBalance Institute, LLC

Visit our website at www.lifebal.net

Design & layout by Myrna Varga, The Office Connection

ISBN: 0-9753586-0-X

First edition published 2004

Printed in the United States of America
LifeBalance Institute Press

10 9 8 7 6 5 4 3 2 1

Leo:

I am so grateful for my wonderful Shirley, who has inspired me, guided me and allowed me to devote a major portion of my time to creating the LifeBalance System. Without her, Heavenly Father and Napoleon Hill, the system would have never been developed. Without Mark Kastleman and Bob Wright, only my few coaching clients would ever have benefited from it. I am truly one very grateful and blessed man.

Mark:

To my beloved companion Ladawn:
You truly are the wind beneath my wings.
To my children, Jared, Joshua, Krystal, Jordan, Jacob and Jason: Thank you for bringing so much joy and wonder into my life, and teaching me how to love unconditionally.
To my dear friend, coach and mentor Leo Weidner for making all of this possible.
To my teacher, Dr. Page Bailey, for unlocking the door and leading me into the breathtaking world of mind-brain science and a lifetime of continual learning and discovery.
To Bob Wright for his great friendship, wonderful insights and significant contributions that
helped give this book a "heart."

CONTENTS

Appendix:

What lies behind us and what lies before us are tiny matters compared to what lies within us.

— *Oliver Wendell Holmes*

ACHIEVING
the Balance

"Leo, how do we give people an easy, simple way to actually implement these things into their daily lives?"

—Dr. Napoleon Hill, 1966

Introduction

The Journey Begins:
Dr. Napoleon Hill issues
a challenge to Leo Weidner

It was fitting that billowing white clouds and a brilliant rainbow accompanied us on that gorgeous morning in 1966. My traveling companion, Dr. Napoleon Hill (author of *Think and Grow Rich*), was explaining how to obtain the proverbial "pot at the end of the rainbow." We drove south along the picturesque Oregon coast. A gentle, early-morning rain had left the air and highway clean and freshly scrubbed. But it wasn't the beauty of the morning that I remember most, rather my overall experience with Dr. Hill. The six hours we spent together seemed a fleeting moment in time as Dr. Hill shared with me his (decades-long) past studies of America's most successful people.

Dr. Hill had been commissioned by Andrew Carnegie, the great American industrialist and founder of U.S. Steel, to conduct a study of Mr. Carnegie's close friends who were America's most successful individuals, including Henry Ford, Charles M. Schwab, Theodore Roosevelt, Wilbur Wright, Thomas Edison, Alexander Graham Bell

1

and many others. For the next 20 years Dr. Hill interviewed, researched and analyzed over 500 of these individuals in a quest to find the key to their success. He told me he spent almost six months with Tom Edison.

"Leo!" he exclaimed, "Did you know that these wealthy and successful Americans had one quality in common?" Before I could respond he continued, "They had committed to paper the goals they wished to accomplish. This written statement became their focus, passion and obsession, the primary vehicle that motivated them to success." He called this written statement of goals a person's Definite Major Purpose.

"Leo," he went on, "I've spent over 20 years interviewing and analyzing America's most successful men, and nearly another 40 years teaching others what I uncovered. I've identified the keys to their success, but, Leo, how do we give people an easy, simple way to actually implement these things into their daily lives?"

From that day forward, I dedicated my life's work to finding a solution to Dr. Hill's challenge.

Over the next two years I rubbed shoulders with this master of success and motivation as I helped him develop the Napoleon Hill Academy. In the academy program, we brought husbands and wives into the classroom environment and, over a 17-week period, taught them the 17 Principles of Success Dr. Hill had formulated from his findings. However, while these wonderful classes were filled with tremendously helpful information, there was something missing: there was no practical implementation system. With his brilliant bestseller *Think and Grow Rich*, and his work at the Napoleon Hill Academy, Dr. Hill laid the foundation for the self-improvement movement that dominated the '40's, '50's and '60's, and is to this day the foundational work that most self improvement goes back to. But I felt it was up to me to build on his work and develop and put into practice a daily implementation system.

Developing the LifeBalance System came as a direct result of applying the core concepts developed by Dr. Hill, and my own conviction that every person already has all of the natural built-in abilities they need to succeed. It became my life's work to develop and teach simple daily tools that would allow everyone to achieve the same levels of success that had come to just a few prominent Americans.

I further realized that helping people achieve success in one specific area of their life, as many of the people Dr. Hill interviewed had done, produces the most positive results when it also takes into account all the significant relationships in a person's life. Out of this grew the concept of LifeBalance. LifeBalance has helped successful people become more successful, and less-than-successful people achieve their dreams.

I am grateful to the clients who have worked with me through the years; the thousands of individuals that helped me develop the insights into these powerful tools. Their success through my program has convinced me that greatness is available to all. Utilizing our unique gifts, each of us has the capacity to find happiness, fulfillment, joy and success in all the relationships and pursuits of our lives. The success of my clients can be your success.

In the almost forty years I have been coaching, the LifeBalance tools have been refined and reinforced. As I began looking for ways to take these concepts to an even broader audience, this book came into being. It's purpose is to move beyond the people who can afford a personal coaching relationship, and to take this proven, step-by-step process to everyone.

3

My relationship with others, including my dear friends Dr. Page Bailey and Mark Kastleman, has further reinforced the concepts that have worked so well for thousands. Their work with *Mind-brain Science* verifies and reinforces the powerful results experienced by thousands of my clients. If you are wondering if this system will work for you and you need an extra push, know this: Science is now discovering what so many of us have known for many years—We each have the capacity to achieve all that we desire. In fact, by our very nature, *we are built to succeed.*

This book provides, for the first time ever, a simple daily system that has been proven in the lives of thousands of people, over many years. It works for them, and it will work for you.

When I first met Leo, I knew his expertise would help me stretch and become a better person in achieving my goals and ambitions, but I had no idea that such great impact and change would occur in my life in such a short period of time.   —T. Johnson

1

This Is For You!

Welcome to *Achieving The Balance*! The fact that you are reading this book tells me you have an interest in improving your life. Perhaps you desire greater fulfillment and success in your business or career. You may be in pursuit of more income, less debt and greater overall financial success. Maybe you seek to improve your marriage and other family relationships. You may want to reduce your stress, lose weight, get in better shape or enhance your health and well-being. Perhaps you have a habit, compulsion or addiction that is holding you back. Some of your dreams may remain unfulfilled, or you may have trouble deciding exactly what you want to do with the rest of your life. Whatever your specific needs and wants may be, you are most likely seeking simple, practical answers that will lead to the happiness and success, you desire. If any of this rings true, then this book is for you!

In today's world, there is no shortage of self-improvement books, programs and gurus, all claiming to have *the* answers. You may have tried one or more of these. But, if you are like most people, within a few weeks of finishing the book, listening to the tapes, or attending the seminar you probably found yourself more or less right back where you started, with the same habits, the same stress, and the same unfulfilled dreams—back in the same old rut. Over the years I have received feedback from thousands of individuals. Perhaps you can relate to a comment recently expressed to me by a new client:

Leo, the ideas I get from the books and tapes are great, and I really want to start living these things in my daily life. But inevitably after a few days or weeks, the initial excitement fades, the books and tapes end up on the shelf, and I find myself right back in the same old rut with the same old habits and ways of thinking. With all the stress and obligations in my life, I just can't seem to find the time or a simple, easy way to put this stuff into practice. I'm tired of always hearing and reading about self-improvement—I want to actually start living it!

Everyday, millions of individuals go about their busy lives, while tucked away in the backs of their minds are dreams and desires for a more successful, fulfilling, and stress-free life. "So," you may be wondering, "What makes this book different from all the others out there? Without any double-talk, detours or beating around the bush, let's get right to the answers.

There are five primary reasons why the *LifeBalance System* is different, unique and will work for you:

Reason #1:
It Has Already Worked For People Just Like You!

As I look back on the thousands of people I have worked with, it's amazing the variety of personalities and backgrounds they represent.

I have coached every possible type of person, and yet they have all succeeded with this system.

This system is not just for self-help gurus. *Achieving The Balance* works for everyone. Their success is your confidence.

Reason #2:
A Simple Daily Implementation Process

A top executive with one of the world's leading self-improvement companies once was asked, "Of the millions of people who buy your book, how many actually read it all the way through?" He promptly replied, "About 8 percent." "And how many of those," came the follow-up question, "actually implement the book's principles into their lives?" His response was telling: "We've done some studies on that and found that only 7 percent of those who read the book all the way through actually practice at least one of the book's principles each week on a consistent long-term basis."

Many hundreds of self-improvement and success titles line the bookstore shelves. Most contain scores of valuable concepts and ideas. But they lack a simple "how to" daily implementation process, i.e., "That's a great idea, but exactly how do I consistently live it in my everyday life?" Good ideas are a dime-a-dozen. How to *consistently* implement them on a daily basis and make them a permanent part of your life is where the greatest value resides.

The LifeBalance System is an *implementation system*. You will learn how-to, on a daily basis, achieve the success, fulfillment, and happiness you desire. From now on any time you read about or hear a new idea, feel an impression, receive an inspiration, or formulate a new goal, you will know exactly *how* to convert it to success in your life. You can also use this system to overcome any negative habits,

7

compulsions, addictions, or specific challenges you have now and in the future.

Too often getting from where you are right now to where you would like to be in your life is like walking a tightrope. The slightest gust of wind or variation off course, and it's off into oblivion. The rope you are balancing on can seem so small, and the objective so far away and difficult to reach. Using the skills you gain in this book you will turn your tightrope into a solid, easy-to-cross bridge. The LifeBalance System is the lifetime vehicle to which you can attach any goal, desire or aspiration to cross the bridge to success.

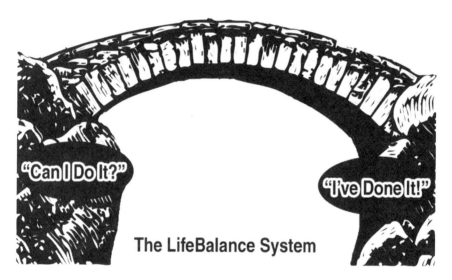

"Can I Do It?"

"I've Done It!"

The LifeBalance System

Reason #3:
Your Own Unique, Individualized System

To some degree we all find ourselves trying to live up to the expectations of others; our parents, spouse, children, employer, friends, colleagues. At times we may look at others and think, "I wish I were more like her," or, "What I wouldn't give to have his success." In fact, many self-improvement programs encourage this tendency by dictating the traits you should seek, defining what *success* is, and pushing you to implement pre-fabricated, one-size-fits-all approaches. But you aren't like anyone else. You are unique in all the world. You have been endowed by your Creator with special gifts, talents and abilities that are yours alone. You have your own personality, challenges, dreams and desires. You need a daily program that is as individual and unique as you are.

Through the LifeBalance System, you learn how to use **3 Basic Tools**: the *Feelings Journal*™, the *LifeCreed*™, and the *Byte*. Utilizing these tools you will discover who you truly are and what you want most, or in other words, *your* ideal self and *your* ideal life. Applying the same tools, you will create your own *custom daily implementation plan* designed to take full advantage of your unique gifts, talents and personality. Where generic, one-size-fits all plans have failed, your highly customized plan guarantees your success.

Reason #4:
Create a Balanced Life

The title of this book is *Achieving The Balance*. What does it mean to have a *balanced life*? If you stop and think about it, every part of your life fits into one or more of *six general categories* called *relationships*, and your success, happiness and fulfillment in life is fully dependent upon the quality of these relationships. The *6 Key Relationships* in your life are:

- *Spiritual*: your relationship with your Creator.
- *Emotional/Intellectual*: your relationship with yourself.
- *Physical*: your relationship with your body—health and fitness.

9

- *Family*: your relationship with your spouse, children and/or other family members.
- *Social*: your relationship with others—friends, neighbors, co-workers, etc.
- *Career/Financial*: your relationship with your job and money.

You probably have things in your life you want to improve, goals you want to achieve, in one of more of these six key relationships. The LifeBalance System will provide you with simple daily tools to make immediate significant progress in those areas of your life that are the most urgent and pressing—those things you want to improve "right now." Through the LifeBalance System you will be able to achieve success in any specific area of your life that you desire. However, you will also learn how to achieve *LifeBalance* in the process. You will learn how to be simultaneously successful in each of the six key relationships in your life.

Can you think of anyone in politics, science, business, sports, entertainment, or in your own family, who has achieved remarkable success in a particular pursuit while failing miserably in other important areas of their life and relationships? Too often, people and programs focus on a singular objective: making money, losing weight, succeeding in business, finding the perfect relationship—all potentially worthy goals. However, too often this narrow focus results in a life terribly out of balance. While the individual may achieve their singular purpose, they often do so at the sacrifice of other equally or more important areas—marriage and child relationships, health, spirituality, friendships, and overall joy and fulfillment in life.

The key to a balanced life, minimized stress, and maximized success and happiness begins with prioritizing your 6 Key Relationships

—putting what matters most, first. This process is unique to the Life-Balance System and in many ways runs counter to other self-improvement programs and to the typical philosophies of the business world. However, the relationship priority process produces astounding results. For example, by prioritizing their relationship with career/money as last, many of my business-owner clients have used this system to double or triple their incomes while reducing their work time by a third.

While you can focus totally on one singular goal and achieve it, if in the process you neglect the other key relationships in your life, you will find yourself constantly running to "put out the next fire" or "fix something else that has broken down." With the LifeBalance System you achieve specific goals and successes *while* keeping all other areas of your life in balance. In a sense, *you can have it all*.

Reason #5:
Harness Your Own Natural
Built-In *Successability*

You already possess everything you need to succeed in every aspect of your life. You have been constantly using this natural built-in *Successability* since the day you were born. Every task you have mastered, every skill you have developed, or in other words, *every habit you have formed*—from the insignificant to the dramatic, positive or negative—are all proof of your highly developed success skills. You have literally achieved hundreds of thousands of *successes* in your lifetime!

Unfortunately, much of the time you are not consciously aware that you are using these natural abilities. Before you realize it a habit has formed. These habits can be positive and productive or they can be negative and destructive. But even your negative habits prove that you have the natural ability to *succeed*.

11

The LifeBalance System uses these natural built-in success mechanisms to form the specific positive habits and achieve the precise outcomes you desire. There are **3 Simple Rules** that control your natural built-in habit-formation processes or Successability. Combining the Three Simple Rules with the Three Basic Tools of the LifeBalance System and applying them to your own unique daily program, you will achieve your highest goals and objectives.

Now that you have a basic understanding of how the LifeBalance System is different and unique from other programs, let's go right to the system itself. We will begin with *Achieving LifeBalance: The Slight Edge*.

After 21 years of study, I can say from the bottom of my heart that nothing comes close to promoting the lasting, balanced change needed for success as does Leo Weidner's Life Balance program.

—J. Naccarato

2

Achieving LifeBalance: The *Slight Edge*

As you begin implementing the Three Simple Rules and Three Basic Tools of the LifeBalance System, you will quickly discover they are amazingly powerful. Virtually any goal, preferred habit, newly discovered self-improvement idea, or other desire for change you articulate and insert into this process, will come to fruition.

The challenge lies in deciding which goals and changes to focus on, and in what order of priority. Many people in our society place "making more money and being more successful" at the top of their priority list. In fact, many of my clients make the following claim:

"Using the LifeBalance System, I doubled my income and cut my work hours by a third."

This is indeed a bold statement, but for many of the 2,000+ people I have personally coached, this claim is a reality. Many have dramatically surpassed these numbers. You're probably wondering, "How did they do it?" I can tell you this: They did not have to work double the hours or doubly hard to earn double the income. The grand key to their success is the *slight edge* they gained through *LifeBalance*.

A brief example taken from the Olympics serves to illustrate this powerful concept:

There they stand on the three-tiered platform, three Olympic medalists, the gold-medal winner atop the highest level, the silver on the next and the bronze on the lowest. The glorious, though fleeting moment passes for the silver and bronze winners, but not for the winner of the gold. Movie contracts, product endorsements, TV commercials, books and articles are poised to make this athlete a millionaire overnight. All this attention would suggest that the winner was overwhelmingly better than the second and third spots. However, the clock shows they were separated by only 11/1000 of a second! A split second, a fraction of an inch, a *slight edge* can make the difference between winning and "also ran."

If you want to enjoy greater success in any area of your life, including significantly increasing your income, you should do everything within your power to gain the slight edge—putting what matters most, first.

This *slight edge* gives you the ability to focus on what truly needs your attention right now, and not be distracted by the other things in your life that are unhealthy or disruptive.

Is your life dying from making a living?

We live in a society that places tremendous focus and value on making money. Out of all the activities in people's lives, many devote the lion's share of time, energy and attention to making money. Many

14

"keep score" by how much they earn or have; the size of their house; the make and model of their car. . . Others, in contrast, struggle just to keep their heads above water.

Regardless of their level of income, in our money-centered society many find they are "dying from making a living." Their marriages, relationships with their children, health, spirituality, and overall love of life are dying. The associated stress is killing them. It doesn't matter whether a person makes $30,000, or $1 million a year, because the components of happiness aren't found in money. In fact, many who achieve the highest monetary success do so at the sacrifice of success in their personal and family lives. Though more than capable of giving and serving in their marriages, families and society, these potentials often go unrealized because making money takes so much of their time and energy.

Recently I read an article about a medical doctor who conducted a survey of 1,200 people with highly successful careers. His survey revolved around two major topics: (1) Did the professionals enjoy their personal/family life? (2) Did they enjoy their work? The responses were very telling: 80% enjoyed their work but did not enjoy their personal/family life. 15% enjoyed neither their personal/family life nor their business life. Only 5% enjoyed both their personal/family life and their work.

LifeBalance = More Financial Success, Less Stress, Better Relationships

Almost all of my clients first hired me as a *LifeBalance Coach* because they heard I could show them how to make more money, or be more productive in their business. Had I initially told them, "I will help you improve your health, marriage, relationships with children, lower your stress and attain LifeBalance," many would've fired back, "I'm not looking for a marriage counselor or fitness trainer, I just want to make more money!" But, once they began implementing the system, all came to understand the most effective way to make more money is through achieving balance in the things that really matter most in one's life.

The key to financial success is creating an environment in your everyday life that allows you to truly FOCUS your attention. When your life is in balance, your mind is clear, at peace—you are productive. Oppositely, when you are constantly preoccupied with worries and stress about money, your marriage, children, health, bills, etc., your productivity and ability to focus are greatly diminished.

Making more money may not have been what brought you to this book, but having any area of your life out of balance and drawing an inappropriate amount of your focus, will lead you to the same place— where the most important relationships in your life pay the price. If you want a better marriage, focus on the things that *truly* matter most in your life and you will achieve it. Want a better relationship with your creator and your faith? Put this relationship in the proper order of focus and balance and you will be successful.

Have you ever tried to carry on a conversation with someone who was preoccupied; whose focus was somewhere else? Have you ever been interrupted while concentrating on a project, and found it difficult to get in the mood and establish your focus all over again? Have you ever gotten into an argument with your spouse, child, co-worker or boss, and then tried to concentrate on your work? Or have you ever been troubled by a major worry, only to find that it dominates your thoughts day and night? The mind cannot focus on two dissimilar things at once. If you are preoccupied with stress and worry, your productivity and ability to succeed, financially or otherwise, is limited.

Many Feel the Stress and Do It Anyway

On considering these concepts, many respond, "I have stress every day—it's just the way it is. I just deal with it and push myself forward." Some even insist they manage just fine financially while dealing with stress and worry at the same time. In limited cases, this may be true, but at what cost?

Years ago when I lived in Oregon, occasionally I would sit and watch the tugboats pushing giant, heavy-laden barges up the Willamette River. Even though the tugs were outfitted with massive diesel engines, the forward progress of the barges was slow and cumbersome, requiring massive amounts of horsepower and fuel to propel them up the river. It seemed as if the tugs and barges were laboring through thick sludge rather than cool, clear water. Yet, had the same tugboat engine been strapped to the hull of a sleek speedboat, the result would've been much different. Are you a tired tugboat struggling to force a stress-filled barge upstream? Or are you a streamlined, power-packed craft roaring upriver heedless of the current?

One of my clients tells the story of a hike he went on as a teen:

"I was with a group of friends on a 50-mile hike in the High Sierras. Several in the group decided to play a joke on me. During our breaks, they put rocks in my backpack—a few at a time. As the day went on, my pack felt heavier and heavier. I assumed it was because I was growing progressively tired with the miles. Then in the mid-afternoon, I discovered the rocks and removed them. I was amazed at the difference in my backpack—it was so light! I immediately went to the front of the group and hiked easily until sunset."

How many of us are weighed down with heavy burdens, pressures, stresses and worries, but, like the hiker, expend tremendous energy trudging ahead anyway? "I'm worried about my marriage, my kids, my health, my bills, but I've got to focus on my work—I can't deal with all these distractions!" So, we push on ahead, but at what cost? Years of "feeling the stress and doing it anyway" can exact a heavy toll on marriages, families, physical and mental health. If we take steps to rid ourselves of these burdens, how much more effective can we be?

What About Those Who Advise, "Focus on making money and that will relieve most of your personal pressures"?

The traditional philosophy that tells us to put our noses to the grindstone and focus on making money is alive and well. When you eliminate all the jargon and fluff, what this philosophy is really saying is "Put making money first in your life and everything else will work out."

In his book *The 7 Habits of Highly Effective People*, Stephen Covey talks about the need for a healthy balance between the goose (production capability) and the golden eggs (production). If the goose is neglected, overworked and driven to produce even more precious eggs, production may go up temporarily, but in the long run, you kill the goose!

Think of yourself as the goose and the money you earn as golden eggs. Push yourself, work long hours, sacrifice nutrition and exercise, neglect your marriage and children, carry heavy burdens of stress and worry—all in the name of more golden eggs—and eventually you'll end up losing what matters most and killing the goose in the process.

Often when my clients begin to get their lives in balance they look back and say, "Leo, my life was dying from making a living and I didn't even know it. My total focus was on money and I was missing out on all the really meaningful things in my life." One client told me, "I'd go to the office with my guts in a knot from an argument with my wife, I was stressed out about my teenage son failing school, I was overweight and out of shape, I was self-medicating with caffeine, food, TV and a lot of other escapes. I was making good money, but my life was a mess. After applying the LifeBalance System it was amazing how different I felt with just a few minor changes."

Wrap Your Business/Career Around Your Personal Life, Not Your Personal Life Around Your Business/Career

An anonymous writer once penned: "Don't ever let what you do for a living become what your are." In today's hectic, push-and-shove, bottom-line-focused business world, that's hard to do. Indeed, most people wrap their personal lives around their businesses/careers.

Take both of your hands and stretch them out in front of you, palms up. Now, form your right hand into a fist. It represents your business/career, while your left hand represents your personal and family life. Now take your open hand and wrap it around your fist. What is at the center or core? The answer is your business/career. With this typical approach, most people end up neglecting what truly matters most in their lives.

Rather than taking this all-too-common approach, I teach my clients to wrap their businesses/careers around their personal lives, placing what matters most to them at the center. As a result of this small yet pivotal adjustment in priority, the reduction of stress and the spike in productivity and personal income are nothing short of astounding.

Balance is not about time: "I spend this much time with my family and this much with work, therefore I'm balanced." It's about having the peace of mind knowing you are putting what matters most in your life first. When you can describe your life with phrases such as: "I exercise, I eat right, I spend quality and quantity time with my spouse and children, I nourish my spiritual nature, I have hobbies I really enjoy, I love my work, I serve and give to others;" then you can with credibility say, "my life is in balance."

When you wrap your business/career around your personal and family life, you tap into hidden stores of energy and lift your attitude at work. Knowing you're taking care of what matters most sets your mind at ease; you are at peace. You're able to concentrate and fully focus on your work. Creativity soars. Your communication and relationships with colleagues, employees and clients improve markedly. Everything in your business/career improves because you have achieved true LifeBalance—you have attained the *slight edge.*

Portrait: Finding Balance in Life

I recently received a testimonial letter from one of my clients. It illustrates the importance of achieving LifeBalance.

"When I first began working with Leo I really didn't know how out of balance my life was. I just figured I was like everyone else— working long hours, stressed, problems at home, out of shape and over- weight, just trying to stay on top. Isn't that the norm? Leo tried to show me where I was out of balance, but I didn't want to see it; I didn't want to admit it. However, when I started keeping my Feelings-Journal and listening to my LifeCreed, I discovered my life was out of balance in a lot of ways."

"So, I decided to start using Leo's system of putting myself, my God and my family first. And as I did, amazing things started happening with my business. It's hard to explain, but I think it comes down to this: When you put the people that really matter most first in your life, you transfer energy and thoughts that say to your clients, employees and co-workers, "I'm a person of integrity and inner strength who really cares about others and not just using them to get power or money—because I put those who matter most first in my life."

"To put it bluntly, you're free from the stress of a wife who thinks you're a jerk, from kids who are out of control and hardly know their dad, from lousy health, etc. When your personal and family life is in order, you can fully focus without distraction on your business. As a result, you start to care about others more and treat and communicate with them better. You feel better about yourself and your life and you become more effective in business. My income went way up and at the same time I was able to spend more time on personal pursuits and my family. I never thought I could do both of these at the same time."

Do you place what matters most at the center of your life? How do you achieve this thing called LifeBalance?

I used to think I had to focus all my attention and energy on making money if I was ever going to get to the top. When I learned how to achieve true balance in my life, my income tripled and my marriage and family life are better than ever. —L. Baldwin

I was so splintered. I was ineffective with both my work and my family. There was no balance in my life. Through Leo's program that has all changed. Achieving The Balance is first class. It has changed my life forever.

—Peter Jeppson

3

Your Six Key Relationships: The *Relationship Pyramid*

∾

True LifeBalance Is All About RELATIONSHIPS

If you truly desire to make more money, reduce stress, increase balance in your life, the grand key is the quality of your relationships. If you truly want to place what matters most at the center, begin focusing on your relationships. I've heard it said that: "Whatever issue you're struggling with, it can always be traced back to a relationship." I promise that if you take care of the key relationships in your life, everything else will fall into place.

In an effort to illustrate the importance of key relationships and their order of priority, I have developed the *Relationship Pyramid*:

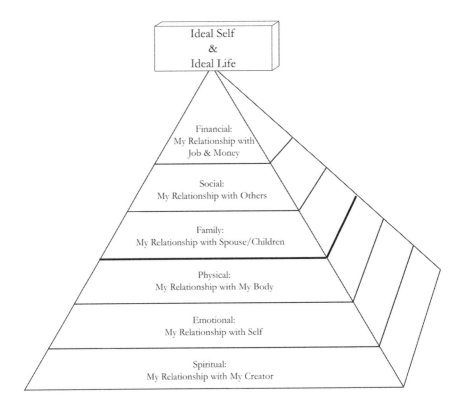

Building from the base up, each relationship offers foundational strength and power to those above it. Only with each level of the pyramid built upon the other, in order, can you reach the top, the realization of your ideal self and your ideal life. If you try to take short cuts or only partially construct the lower levels (i.e., putting the financial relationship first or giving it the major focus), the resulting pyramid is skewed, off-kilter and will eventually collapse.

⌒

Let's briefly examine the building blocks of the Relationship Pyramid.

Spiritual—My Relationship with my Creator: This relationship needs to come before all others. When you are spiritually in-tune, balanced and connected, you possess an inner peace and strength that ripples through all other relationships and circumstances in your life. When you establish a strong relationship with things spiritual, everything else in your life falls into place.

Emotional—My Relationship with Self: Under the time constraints of job, family and myriad other commitments, many of us find it easy to neglect our relationship with self, which comprises strengthening and increasing our emotional and intellectual capacities. One of the most powerful concepts covered in this book is that of mind-brain science, best conveyed by the statement, "As a man thinketh, so is he."

Your thoughts, feelings and especially your self-talk at any given moment govern how much success you experience in business, marriage, family and every other aspect of your life. In other words, your inner world dictates your outer world. Like many people, you can simply be reactive, allowing your thoughts and emotions to be dictated by the current dominant circumstance or situation, which in turn will dictate the quality of your life and relationships. Or, conversely, you can learn how to proactively, purposefully direct your thoughts and emotions exactly as you choose in any given situation to produce the specific results you want most.

Physical—My Relationship with My Body: In our hectic, busy lives one of the first relationships we neglect and/or abuse is the relationship we have with our bodies. Exhausted from long hours at work, family pressures and the overall stress of life, exercise is often the last thing on our priority list. We often procrastinate, or bypass it altogether. After a long day it's hard to get oneself motivated for five sets each of, ab crunches, pull-ups and push-ups. And we don't have time to jog in the morning because "I have so much to do today." Armed with so many excuses, at the end of the day we often just fall on the couch and vegetate in front of the TV.

Likewise, our fast-paced society makes us prone to reach for fast food rather than go to the trouble of seeking out fresh, nutritional alternatives. In social settings, we eat what others are having. And at night, while crashed on the couch, we consume more junk food. Such abuse seriously weakens our bodies, saps our energy, dampens our attitude, and generally erodes our health and well-being. If your relationship with your body isn't right, it will have an adverse effect on virtually every other area of your life, including your ability to be successful in your business or career.

You Must Serve Yourself First

I've used a bold line on the pyramid to separate the first three relationships: Spiritual, Emotional/Intellectual and Health/Fitness, from the other three. The quality of the first three relationships is essential to your success in every other relationship and aspect of your life. In order to achieve the highest level of success in your marriage, family, social life and career, **you must serve yourself first**. Many have conditioned themselves to believe they "don't have time" or "it's not a top priority" to worry about spirituality, emotional/intellectual recharging, or fitness and nutrition. Others genuinely try to get around to these priorities, but do so sporadically or not at all. Choosing any of these approaches will only end up costing them in the end. Some may neglect these critical relationships and still manage to make lots of money, but again, at what cost?

When I think of neglecting the first three relationships, I think of a laptop computer receiving its operating power from an internal battery. When the battery is close to being drained, the computer sounds a "battery low" warning to signal the need for a recharge. If the user ignores the warning, the battery continues to drain; higher computer functions soon begin to fail until the system finally shuts down completely.

Are we sometimes like a laptop? When our spiritual, mental/emotional or health/fitness batteries are running low certain warning signs appear: fatigue, depression, anxiety, stress, frequent illness, anger, relationship problems, and the list goes on. If we ignore these warnings our higher functions begin to shut down until, finally, our whole system fails: heart attack, cancer, bankruptcy, divorce, broken relationships with children, angry colleagues, dissatisfied employees, addiction…

Recharge your spiritual, emotional/intellectual and health/fitness batteries every day. Don't allow them to drain to dangerously low levels. Put these foundational relationships first, and your top-of-the-pyramid family, social and career/money relationships will all fall into place. And you will be a success, measured not by earnings and possessions, fame or power, but by the deep relationships you've forged with God, self, and family.

Family—My Relationship with my Spouse and Children: A great man once said: "No success [no matter how great] can compensate for failure in the home." We live in a society where the earnest pursuit of wealth frequently takes precedence over marriage; the thirst for recognition overshadows family. Most husbands and wives don't get up in the morning and say to themselves, "Today I'm going to go out and neglect my spouse and children." People just get so caught up in the busyness and urgency of life that, by default, they end up neglecting those they care most about.

I believe we were created to derive our greatest joy from serving first, our husband or wife, then our children. And I believe the greatest gift we can give our children is allowing them to observe us loving and serving our mate. Unfortunately, in the rush of building a career we can miss out on those once-in-a-lifetime opportunities to experience this remarkable joy.

Social—My Relationship with Others: As you place the first four relationships first in your life, you will find a dramatic improvement in your relationships with everyone else. Your attitude will change for the better. You will find it easier to be warm, friendly and enthusiastic. Others will sense your positive aura, feel your energy and be drawn to you. You will develop greater richness in your relationships with employees, co-workers, colleagues, clients, friends, extended family—everyone you meet.

Financial—My Relationship with My Career and Money: If you will take care of—in order of priority—the five key relationships listed above, I promise that your relationship with money and your job will be enhanced in ways that will astound you. Like so many of my clients, you will evolve to the point where you can double (or more) your income while reducing your work hours by a third, if you are in an entrepreneurial environment. If you earn a salary or wage, you will find yourself gaining remarkable opportunities for growth and advancement. I'm not suggesting you won't have to work at it. But, if you will attend to the other five key relationships in the pyramid, your overall effectiveness and performance in your career will significantly increase. You will be able to do more, do it more effectively, and do it in less time. Your ability to deal with the challenges and difficult issues spawned by the business world will be strengthened while your worries and stress fade away.

Understanding the critical importance of putting what matters most, first, and what true LifeBalance is all about, you are now ready to begin using the Three Rules and the Three Tools.

Now It's Your Turn

Your *LifeBalance Workbook*

Obtain a 3-ring binder and fill it with at least 50 sheets of lined paper. This binder is your *LifeBalance Workbook*. At the end of many of the chapters in this book is a section titled, *Now It's Your Turn*. In each of these sections are special exercises. You will use your LifeBalance Workbook to record your work with these exercises. The exercises are designed to help you in four significant ways:

1. .Each exercise is designed to give you hands-on practical use of one or more of the Three Tools. When you immediately and directly apply the new knowledge you have gained, your comprehension, retention and confidence in the use of each tool will increase dramatically.

2. Each exercise is designed to generate immediate positive changes in the quality of your life, success and relationships.

Experiencing these immediate results will motivate you to continue discovering and implementing each tool in the LifeBalance System.

3. Very importantly, each completed exercise will provide you with valuable resources for the creation and continued revision of the most powerful document in your life; the *LifeCreed*. You will find through the exercises completed and recorded in your Workbook, a significant amount of preparation work on your LifeCreed will have been completed.

4. Your LifeBalance Workbook will contain a written record of your work with all of the *Now It's Your Turn* exercises. The LifeBalance Workbook will be a valuable reference for all you have learned and experienced.

Exercise

Take a piece of paper from your LifeBalance Workbook to create your own Relationship Pyramid.

Filling up as much space on your sheet of paper as possible, sketch a copy of the pyramid. Your pyramid should look just like the one in the book, but **blank, without any words**. (If you prefer to print out a copy of the blank pyramid, please visit the LifeBalance Institute website at www.lifebal.net and click on the "Resource" section.)

In the first blank section at the bottom of the pyramid write in the name of your Creator. In the next section up, write in your name. In the third blank section write in a brief description of your ideal physical body: weight, fat percentage, fitness level, etc. In the section above that write the name of your spouse and each of your children. If you're not married or don't have children, write the name(s) of your most significant family member(s). In the fifth section write the names of your most important friends, colleagues, employees, etc. In the top section, write in the name of your business, career or position. Finally, in the box balancing on the top of the pyramid write "My Ideal Self and My Ideal Life."

Make a copy of your finished pyramid. Take the original and put it in your LifeBalance Workbook. Take the copy of your Relationship Pyramid and put it in a prominent place like the bathroom mirror, fridge, next to your computer, etc., where you can review it every day. It will remind you to put what matters most, first and it will give you the slight edge you've been searching for.

Thanks for bringing me out of the unconscious spaces where I've lived most of my life, and into the conscious realm—the Privileged Place!
—*L. Ritchie*

4

You Are Already Built For Success!
The Three Simple Rules

After being introduced to the concept of "every person possessing a natural built-in *Successability*," one LifeBalance client made this observation: "I agree that I have achieved some successes in my life. But a lot of the goals I set never seem to work out. All the years I've made New Year's Resolutions I can only think of a few I've followed through with. I've read lots of self-improvement books and I love the ideas but I don't live most of them. I'm still overweight and I still have struggles in my marriage. I'd love to make a lot more money but it doesn't happen. So if I have this so-called natural Successability, why hasn't it worked?"

The answer is, "It has."

When most people think of the word "success," they think of making more money, building a profitable business enterprise, excelling in academics, music, athletics or achieving some other "positive" result. But success in its most complete definition is simply the outcome, good or bad, of your consistent thoughts and actions—your habits. Every habit you have is proof of your ability to succeed! You have been *succeeding* every day since the moment of your birth. The question then is not whether you possess this built-in *Successability*, but rather "how does it work and how do you harness and direct it to form the positive habits and achieve the goals you desire most in your life?"

Habits vs. Goals: A Competition

Have you ever enthusiastically set a goal and declared, "This time I'm really going to do it," only to find within a few weeks that in the routine of life the goal just fades away? Why does this happen? Why is it so difficult to set and achieve certain goals in our lives? The reason is quite simple: Whenever you set a goal to behave differently than you have in the past, you immediately set up a **competition** between your goal and your existing dominant habits.

When we speak of our natural built-in Successability, what we are really referring to is our mind-brain's amazing capacity to form habits. Most everything you do in your life is based on your habits.

Note: The term *mind-brain,* refers to the fact that your mind and your brain are separate and distinct but also fully integrated; constantly influencing and altering each other. For detailed review of the mind-brain, please see the Mind-brain Science Appendix at the back of the book.

The first thing to understand about habits is that your mind-brain has one primary focus above all others—to be *efficient*. Why? Think of a few simple skills you learned as a small child: walking, talking, tying your shoes, and riding a bike. At first, you expended tremendous effort and energy to learn these skills. But over time they became easier and more "automatic." This is what your mind-brain seeks—to master a skill as quickly and efficiently as possible until it becomes automatic —a habit. As soon as it has been turned into a habit, your mind-brain can move on to learn and master the next skill. This is how we continually learn, grow and progress.

Imagine what would happen if every time you tried to walk, speak, tie your shoes or engage in any other already-learned skill, you had to master it all over again? What if every time you got in your car to drive somewhere you had to stop and think, "Now what does this pedal do again and what are these knobs and buttons for?" Were it not for the power of habits, you wouldn't get very far in life. Your mind-brain is *habitual* by its very nature—habit is its number one goal. It seeks to turn everything you do into a habit. Because your mind-brain expends such enormous amounts of time and effort to form habits (to be efficient), it guards them very jealously—it doesn't give them up easily.

Each time you set a goal to behave or do something differently in your life and you find yourself slipping back into old habits, it isn't because you are incapable, unintelligent or a failure. Given the opportunity, your mind-brain will choose the path of least resistance—the easiest way to get something done—every single time. Why? Because doing so is efficient! The more activities there are that can be put on autopilot—turned into habits—the more energy and attention your mind-brain has to focus on new challenges and new learning opportunities. Again, the fact that you have so many dominant habits is proof that you have a natural built-in Successability that works incredibly well!

35

Taking all of this into consideration, is it reasonable to assume that just because you get excited about a new self-improvement concept or a new goal, your mind-brain is going to give up the life-long habits it has worked so hard to form? Every time you set a goal you also set up a competition with your existing habits. If you are going to win this competition, you must learn the rules of the game.

The Three Simple Rules of Habit-Formation and Goal Achievement

The latest mind-brain science confirms what I have observed with thousands of clients: that every individual's natural Successability— the ability to form specific habits that lead to the achievement of specific goals—is based on *Three Simple Rules*.

Rule #1:

Clearly state your goal and motive in a way that accesses *mental models* with powerful *meaning.*

Your mind-brain has an amazing built-in automatic process that takes everything you have every experienced and "links" or "connects" these memories together to form what are called *mental models*. These mental models are the *filters* or *glasses* through which you interpret and give *meaning* to everyone and everything around you. Your mind-brain wants to put everything into context. It wants to know "what does this *mean*? The only way your mind-brain can determine the context or meaning of anything is by filtering it through one of your existing mental models. As you read the following phrases, pause with each one to notice the images, thoughts and feelings that come to you:

36

Bill Clinton	My Mother-In-Law
The World Trade Center	High School
My First Kiss	Throwing Up

What kinds of memories, images, and feelings came to the surface? As you read each phrase it was instantly routed to and filtered through a specific mental model. The mental model contains links or connections to everything you have ever experienced that can be associated with the specific phrase. Based on your mental model, you respond to the phrase in a specific way: anger, disgust, fear, fondness, or a combination of many different feelings and emotions. Some mental models become extremely dominant and powerful, resulting in "automatic" responses. From these dominant mental models come what are known as *habits*—the process of responding to the same thoughts, impulses, people, situations or stimulus in the same way every time. Think of some of your dominant habits and the mental models they flow from.

What is it that makes some mental models more powerful and dominant than others? The answer is **MEANING!**

Use *Meaning* to Your Advantage

Advertisers use the mind-brain science of *meaning* constantly, attempting to trigger certain mental models and emotions to sell you their products. For example, have you ever watched a tire commercial where suddenly sitting in the middle of the black rubber tire is a cute, chubby little baby? What does a baby have to do with an automobile tire? Not much. The point is if you viewed the tire alone, the mental model and meaning it activated would be very weak. However, add the baby to the picture and what happens to the mental model and its emotional links?

37

Advertisers link images of sex, money, fame, power, fast cars, exotic locations, attractive people and other unrelated images to their products. Why? Because when you have a need or desire that can be satisfied by a particular product, often the advertised brand that triggers the most powerful mental models and resulting emotions will come to your mind. Advertisers understand how to use this principle: *The mental model with the most powerful meaning wins.*

Advertisers have learned to duplicate what your mind-brain does naturally. In any given situation, how you react or respond is determined by the most dominant mental model, the one with the most powerful *meaning.* When you express a need or desire, your mind-brain will seek the easiest and most efficient way possible to fill that need or desire. It will access the mental model with the most powerful *meaning.*

If you are going to pit a new goal against an existing dominant habit, and win the competition, then you must *clearly state your goal and motive in a way that accesses mental models with powerful meaning.* There are Three Basic Tools you will use on a daily basis to create mental models with powerful meaning: the *Feelings Journal, LifeCreed,* and *The Byte.* These tools will help you harness something that your mind-brain already does naturally, something you have been doing all of your life. But with the Three Basic Tools you will consciously direct the process and produce the specific outcomes you desire. Rather than being a passenger, you will take charge in the driver's seat.

Rule #2:

Engage in Daily Practice and Repetition in the *Privileged Place*

Most of your dominant mental models and the habits that flow from them have been formed over years, or in some cases, over a lifetime of constant practice and repetition. In addition to meaning, repetition also plays a major role in the power of mental models. The more a mental model is accessed and activated over time, the more powerful it becomes—its emotional connections increasing in number and strength. Doing the same thing over and over again forms powerful habits, bringing the activity or behavior to the point where you don't have to consciously think about it any more. This is another way your mind-brain fulfills its priority of efficiency. If the new mental models and habits you desire are to become dominant, you must find an easy and effective way to generate the same type of daily practice and repetition that formed the powerful mental models and habits you are trying to replace.

"But how," you may be wondering, "can I possibly replicate years of practice and thousands of repetitions? I don't have the time for hours of practice every day! And even if I did it would take years to do what you're describing!"

The answer: "By doing a few simple things each day in the *Privileged Place.*

The Privileged Place

Don't be discouraged by the concept of daily practice and repetition. There is a way to "short-cut" the process, forming your new mental models and habits without investing the same amount and duration of repetition that formed your old ones. But, this can only be accomplished in what is known as the *Privileged Place.*

Imagine you're standing on the shore looking out over the vast ocean. You can't see the billions of activities going on under the surface; they are invisible to you. This represents the unconscious level of your mind-brain, where things take place automatically, "below the surface of the water." These include life-sustaining processes as well as habits. You may find your life dictated by mental models and habits operating at this unconscious level, activated over and over again. You may be stuck in the same old behavioral cycle, living a circular life. In a circular life, you live as a slave to your existing dominant mental models and unproductive habits, going around and around on the same track. In the confines of the circle, your options are extremely limited.

Now imagine as you're looking out over the ocean and your attention is suddenly drawn to an object breaking through the surface of the water. This represents something coming into your conscious thoughts or entering what my colleague Dr. Page Bailey calls the *Privileged Place.* Your consciousness is a Privileged Place because only there can you direct the formation of new mental models and habits that will override your old ones.

The **Privileged Place is a place of enormous power.** Using the Three Basic Tools—*Feelings Journal, LifeCreed* and *Byte*—you will harness this power and use it to accelerate the daily practice and repetition required to form new mental models and habits, and achieve your goals. What was once thought impossible, or at the least required years of concentrated effort, can now be achieved in remarkably short periods of time. When you purposely direct the achievement of your goals from the Privileged Place, they become what are called *Consciously Directed Goals*. These goals are dramatically different from the traditional New Year's Resolutions, goals posted on the refrigerator or bathroom mirror, or goals listed in your daily calendar or PDA. When you begin pursuing Consciously Directed Goals, you can expect consistently remarkable success.

Rule #3:

Give Yourself and Others Permission to Hold You Accountable

In the hectic busyness and stress of everyday life it's very easy to slip below the surface, to the unconscious level, and revert to "auto-pilot"—passively reacting out of old mental models and habits. Give yourself and special people in your life permission to remind you and hold you accountable to consistently spend productive time and effort in the *Privileged Place*.

Within you is a natural built-in Successability. Now, for perhaps the first time, you will learn how to harness and direct this power from the Privileged Place to achieve the specific results you desire most. In the remaining chapters of this book, you will be introduced to and be fully trained in the use of Three Basic Tools that will make it easy for you to fully implement all components of the Three Simple Rules described above. You will take full control of the mental model and habit formation processes and begin your journey toward your ideal self and your ideal life.

Note: This chapter has presented an extremely brief overview of the mind-brain science that provides a scientific explanation and

verification for the effectiveness of the LifeBalance System. **Please
see the *Mind-brain Science Appendix* for a full review.**

5

The Bunker Bean Effect: Discovering and Reaching Your Full Potential

❧

In casual conversation with adult family members, friends or colleagues, how many times have you heard someone say, "I'm still trying to figure out what I want to do when I grow up"? Some of the first questions for new clients are: "What is your vision of your ideal life—what does it look like?" "If you won the lottery tomorrow and money was no longer an issue, how would you spend your time?" The most common responses are "I'm not sure," or "I've never really thought about it."

It is easy to place limitations on yourself based on what you believe you can or can't do. You may also allow family, friends, peers and associates to define and limit you based on who they think you are and what they believe you should be or do. Who are you really? What can you accomplish? What is your ideal self and ideal life?

43

Over the years, many clients have received great inspiration from the following little story known as *The Bunker Bean Effect*. It is a wonderful parable about the greatness within each one of us, and how we can utilize the power of the LifeBalance System to become all that we are meant to be.

The Bunker Bean Effect

"Bunker Bean!" The mystic spoke with authority, "You are the reincarnated Napoleon Bonaparte, conqueror of the world!" Bunker Bean stood in amazement. Timidly he asked, "How could I, who am afraid even of my own shadow, have been the feared and courageous Napoleon?"

Harry Leon Wilson, who in 1912 penned the novel Bunker Bean, says it all started when Bunker Bean became an orphan as a small child. Alone and poor, always dressed in ragged clothes that hung loosely from his small frame, he was mocked and taunted by cruel, merciless children. Fear greeted him when he awoke in the morning and remained his constant companion until sleep put it to rest. He was afraid of everything: elevators, dogs, children, grownups, policemen, situations, the future, life—and even himself.

One fateful day a mystic moved into the cheap, rat-infested boarding house and rented the room next to Bunker Bean. A friendship developed during the next few weeks. The mystic's preoccupation with a book on reincarnation captured Bunker's imagination. He learned that his new friend believed that all people had had previous lives as someone else before being born into their present lives.

The more Bunker Bean thought about this new idea, the more he believed it. One evening after dinner the mystic proclaimed that he and he alone could see into the past and could tell who Bunker Bean was in his past lives. A small pittance of money, which Bunker could ill afford, was delivered to the mystic for the declaration. Bunker followed the mystic to his room and after a few minutes of incantations and trance-producing gyrations, his friend loudly proclaimed:

"Bunker Bean!" The mystic spoke with authority, "You are the reincarnated Napoleon Bonaparte, conqueror of the world!" Bunker Bean stood in amazement. Timidly he asked, "How could I, who am afraid even of my own shadow, have been the feared and courageous Napoleon?"

The mystic explained that life goes in cycles. "Sometimes you are born during the upper part of the cycle and sometimes during the lower part. Napoleon lived on the upper part when he exhibited the qualities of courage, initiative, strength, determination, and power." Bunker Bean then learned that his present life was the result of being born during the lower part of the cycle.

Depressed, he turned to leave; but the mystic yelled in a high-pitched voice, "Bunker, the lower part of the cycle is almost completed! You are now reentering the upper part, the same part you were in when you were Napoleon!" The mystic assured Bunker that it would not be many days before he would feel a change taking place and know the prediction was true. "Even as we speak, you are on your way to becoming courageous, determined, strong, self-reliant, fearless, successful," whispered the mystic.

The very thought that he was once Napoleon caused him to stand a little straighter. By the end of the first day he could even detect hints of the promised change. Now that he thought about it, there was a certain majesty in his look; he began to take on a certain warrior air. When he thought of his "true" identity—Napoleon—he vibrated with a strange new power and determination.

Bunker Bean spent every spare moment reading books about Napoleon. He hung the great general's pictures in the little dirty attic room where he could feast his mind upon his former self. He tried standing, thinking, and acting like Napoleon. The image never left his mind. Even when he was confronted with fear he merely thought, "How would Napoleon feel and what would he do?" and the fear vanished.

He discovered that Napoleon was a master strategist, winning his battles in his tent. Bunker decided he, too, would plan, organize, and think out problems before facing them. He thought of every fear, obstacle, challenge, and danger he might face during the day and determined how Napoleon would react.

Like Napoleon he made sure nothing was left to chance.

The large, colored picture of Napoleon was a constant reminder to Bunker of the great power and strength hidden in his breast. He visualized himself leading and directing vast armies. He vividly imagined the smell of gunpowder, smoke, and blood.

Something strange began to happen to Bunker Bean. He started acting like Napoleon. He forgot his timidity, his fears, and his meager existence. Each challenge was faced with, "How would Napoleon handle it?" He began applying the same principles that made Napoleon great. His fellow workers and employer were amazed at the change in his personality. His boss gave him a more responsible position. Bunker Bean began to feel and be successful.

Not only did Bunker Bean change, but he was amazed at the way people were reacting to him. They wanted to be near him and even followed him as they would a leader. Seeing the changes in these people suggested to him that they might know his real identity.

Years went by and Bunker Bean continued his rise in life and fortune. But one day, when he was pondering over his greatness as Napoleon, he thought, "Before Napoleon who was I"? He searched for and found his old friend and inquired of him. "That will cost you greatly!" said the mystic. "Money is no problem now; just tell me."

The answer he received did not disappoint him. Before he was Napoleon, he was the greatest ruler the world had ever known. He was Ramses, the mighty Egyptian pharaoh. Bunker learned that as Ramses he was tall and handsome and dressed meticulously. Bunker hired a professional tailor to fit him in such a way as to enhance his physical characteristics. His new clothes made him feel like a king and so he began acting like a king. He stood tall, expanded his chest, drew in his waist, and stood erect. He worked to develop the physical and mental discipline of Ramses. He had already discovered that it takes a vivid mental image along with the matching behavior to bring to the present the great qualities of the past. He was a king and must, therefore, do as kings do. Money, for example, was not an issue, because kings always have as much as they want. Bunker knew that when money was needed it would be available, and it was. He was becoming a wealthy man. Bunker Bean was invited to direct large organizations. He was a leader because he thought like a leader and acted like a leader. Never again would he be afraid of life, policemen, mockery, or himself. He was the mighty pharaoh of Egypt. He was born to be a king. His destiny was to rule and so he would do those things that characterized greatness.

The mental image grew stronger with each passing day and in direct proportion strength, vitality, and excitement for life surged through his veins. Not only had he been the courageous, mighty Napoleon, but also the strong, calm, and powerful Ramses. He was a combination of them both. He thought courage at night and awoke in the morning with a giant's strength. His visualization poured the nutrients into his personality to mold and fashion a king and a conqueror.

But one morning tragedy entered Bunker Bean's life; tragedy that neither Napoleon nor Ramses could combat. He discovered that his mystic friend was a fake, a con artist. There really was no such thing as reincarnation. He really hadn't been Napoleon or Ramses. He really was nothing more than his weak, timid, fearful, insignificant self.

Bunker Bean was a beaten man for a few moments. Then, as if by revelation, he thought, "When I believed myself to be a king others reacted as if I were a king. When I believed myself to be weak and timid others reacted as if I were weak and timid."

A new and inspiring truth now dawned upon him. "I can be anything I can imagine and visualize in my mind." During the years he had believed himself to be the reincarnated Napoleon and Ramses, he had accumulated great wealth and position, yet no one had known about his belief except his mystic friend. He had gained all by believing that he could do it. He believed in himself and his dreams. Ramses and Napoleon were only crude bits of scaffolding on which he had climbed to success.

As you begin applying the Three Basic Tools in your daily life, don't sell yourself short when it comes to identifying your ideal self and ideal life. Like Bunker Bean, believe in these great truths:

> Everyone is born a king.
>
> Everyone is born to riches.
>
> Everyone is born to greatness.

Now it's Your Turn

Exercise:

Think of the person in your life, in history, in scripture, in business, etc., that you admire most; that you want to be most like. Visualize this person clearly in your mind. Now, on a blank sheet of paper in your *LifeBalance Workbook*, describe the following about this person:

1. List the specific qualities he or she possesses that you would like to make your own. Next to each quality, state why it is important to you and how it would make your life better if you possessed it.

2. Describe aspects of their personal appearance, health, fitness, communication and social skills you want to emulate. Next to each one state why you want it in your own life.

3. What aspects of their behaviors as a father, mother, husband or wife would you like to incorporate into your own family life? Next to each behavior state how it would improve your family relationships.

4. What have they accomplished in business, career, financially, intellectually, etc., that you want to accomplish? Next to each success, state why you want it in your own life.

Keep the detailed responses from this exercise in your LifeBalance Workbook. At the appropriate time, you will learn how to incorporate many of these things into your own LifeCreed and work toward making them a reality.

One of the most helpful elements I am learning from the LifeBalance System is the habit of writing my feelings on a regular basis and then feeding these into my LifeCreed. I'm so excited to discover who I am, how I really feel, what things I truly value and deeply believe. I am more focused on and concerned about building trusting relationships and nurturing and validating others—particularly my wife, children and clients. . . For me this is what the LifeBalance program is all about—finding that 'zowie' where all the pieces start coming together and working like a symphony. —M. Johnson

It all begins with daily journaling—the ideas, hopes, dreams, confusions—it all comes out. As I journal, I unbury some of my deepest feelings and desires. Journaling is the key! Because you do not hide from yourself. It helps self honesty. It eliminates surprises. Journaling reveals yourself to yourself. —S. Ellis

6

Tool #1: The Feelings Journal™

It's unfortunate that there isn't a better term to describe the *Feelings Journal*. It seems from the beginning it has two strikes against it. First, many people have become proficient at avoiding any mention of feelings, and second a journal sounds like some teeny-bopper diary, and who wants to do that?

First let's consider feelings. Many of us are completely comfortable talking in general terms about feelings. We "hate" broccoli, "love" that song, and "feel" intensely about whoever currently occupies the White House. But put us in a room and ask us to write our feelings, and we panic. Doing so can be awkward and uncomfortable. To avoid the difficulty of the exercise or the potential pain, we convince ourselves that some things are just better left buried and unsaid. The most

51

disappointing aspect of this approach is the assumption that if we avoid it, it doesn't affect us. Nothing could be further from the truth.

If there is one concept you take from reading this book, one tool that would change your life and your relationships, this tool, the Feelings Journal, is it.

It's easy to think that by not bringing it up, the emotional baggage that we carry around will not intrude on our lives. But consider the following experience. It's just one of myriad examples mentioned by clients over the years.

"I'd had a really hard day at work. Nothing particularly out of the ordinary, just the struggles that come along with dealing with customers, traffic, etc. But I was unprepared for what was waiting at home. As I walked in the door, I heard my daughter and son arguing. I entered the room to find them bickering about what to watch on television. That was it, I blew up. I yelled at them both to stop being selfish and sent them to their rooms, forever. They tried to protest, but I wasn't having any of it. Off to bed, no dinner, no television, and no luck."

"I wish I could say this was unusual, but unfortunately, it was all too common. I often seem to react out of proportion to the situation. Events seem to carry me away at times, and I just look back and wonder, 'What was that all about?'"

This client expresses a common behavior. The old "leave well enough alone" approach often places us in situations where we are emotionally unprepared to deal with the slightest stress. The anxieties and unresolved issues in our lives demand attention. They often lurk in the shadows of our consciousness, waiting for an outlet. Without attention, our thoughts and our feelings will find a way out, often resulting in negative consequences.

Feelings Journaling allows us to create a more appropriate context and outlet for our feelings. As we define and distill these feelings, they typically become less overwhelming. We see them for who they are: Oz behind the curtain, pulling the levers on our emotions and responses. Through Feelings Journaling we can choose the time, setting and duration of the experience. Feelings Journaling is the most proactive thing in the LifeBalance System. It will allow you to take control of feelings that always seem to control you. By taking charge of how and when your feelings are expressed, you take control of your own future.

One of my clients had experienced a tremendous amount of personal turmoil. She went through a divorce and was extremely unhappy and discouraged. As she was learning the LifeBalance System, it was easy to see she was really struggling with the program. Finally, one day she came in and declared, "This is my last day. I love the concepts of this program, but it's just not working for me."

As we discussed her situation, two things came to the forefront. First, she hadn't been journaling, and second, she had no dreams, no real hopes for herself. The two were related. When asked about her dreams, she shook her head, "My Dad never believed in dreams, he was very practical." Imagine this comment from a middle-aged woman!

"Dreams are the driving force for good in our lives. They provide the catalyst and the motivation to build a brighter future," I explained. She was still doubtful, but finally agreed to write in her Feelings Journal for just 5 minutes a day, for six of the next seven days. After one week, she reported, "I've Feelings Journaled every day for the last week and I'm so excited!" Through journaling she discovered that she really wanted a change in her job, something she had secretly desired for some time but had buried her feelings out of fear. With her new insight and courage, she made her request and the new position was made available to her. In addition, as a result of journaling she was feeling increased hope in a new relationship, and was becoming excited about her future.

What was the difference? She had taken time to think about herself, to get in touch with her true feelings, and through journaling was forced to put it into writing. Writing allows us to quantify, be specific, and process our feelings and thoughts on a whole new level. Feelings are brought to the conscious level, the *Privileged Place*, and held there while we define them and put them into writing. We take charge, and control the when and where our feelings are expressed. With this approach there are fewer surprises, and we are better able to deal with situations as they really are, without the baggage and without reacting irrationally. Others see us as more stable and consistent, and we are able to deal with difficult situations more appropriately.

You have permission to dream, so dream big! The great scientist Michael Faraday said, "Nothing is too wonderful to be true." Feelings Journaling is the perfect venue to discover your dreams and ambitions, and as a result, your ideal self. Think of it as time spent with the advisor who knows you best—you! Inspiration will come to you as you reflect on your feelings about your relationships, your family, your goals, and even your dreams.

Secondly, we come to the Feelings Journal tool itself. This isn't a diary or log—"I came, I saw, I went, I did," nor is it a history for someone else to read. It is personal, deeply personal. And it is for your eyes only. It is the opportunity for you to spend time in the Privileged Place receiving a host of marvelous benefits, including building new mental models, habits and working toward the achievement of your highest goals. It will be the most important tool you learn to use as you move through the LifeBalance System. Negative feelings will begin to resolve, and positive/hopeful ones will take prominence. Dreams will become clearer, and a new future will begin to surface, which with the added use of the LifeCreed and Byte, will become a reality.

Here's the challenge: Take 5 minutes each morning and write your feelings. Do it for six of the next seven days. You'll see the difference.

Some people, especially men, have difficulty expressing their emotions. At first, this exercise may seem awkward or uncomfortable. Keep in mind that writing in your Feelings Journal is one of the most powerful *Privileged Place* mind-brain exercises you can engage in. Many clients, male and female alike, have used their Feelings Journal to substantially increase their income, dramatically improve their most important relationships, and increase overall success in every aspect of their lives. Just give it a chance, and you will achieve similar results.

Feelings Journaling: A Journey of Discovery

In your busy, hectic life you probably rarely stop and spend quality time pondering a vision of your ideal self and ideal life. In survival mode, the tendency is to focus only on the next task at hand as you push forward in the daily grind. In addition, over your lifetime you have formed many mental models and expectations based on what others —parents, friends, teachers, spouse, colleagues—have thought you should be or do. How can you sift through all of this to discover and clearly articulate your vision of your ideal self and life? It is a journey of discovery. It doesn't all come at once. It requires time and patience as you peel back one layer after another to discover more and more about who you truly are and what you really want.

A client shared the following story:

"While still a senior in high-school, I decided to join the US Navy. My father was in the Navy, my Grandfather had been, as well as my Uncle. It seemed a natural thing to do. I took the placement test required of all new recruits and was told I could choose any field I wanted. I had always loved electronics, and so I chose the Advanced Electronics Field where I could learn to be a missile technician. I enlisted with a friend from school as well, and we were set to go to boot camp and school together.

About a month before graduation, I was sitting in Chemistry class when another recruiter showed up. He began telling us about the Nuclear Power field and stated that it was the most difficult training the Navy had. Only about half of the people who started successfully completed the training. That was all I needed to hear—that it was the hardest thing. I immediately applied, was accepted and spent 8 years as a nuclear electrician on US Navy submarines. Why did I change my mind? Because I thought taking the hard route would make others proud of me; my parents, my grandparents, and friends. I had never learned what my dreams were. I was going through life allowing the opinion of others to define what my goals were. After just a few short months of working with the LifeBalance System, I was able to under-stand what I wanted, what my dreams were, and then begin to achieve them."

As you begin this journey of discovery, keep in mind that your ideal today may be very different from your vision of the ideal a year from now, or three years from now. By way of your Feelings Journal and your LifeCreed, your vision will evolve. You will discover new things about yourself; your gifts and talents, new interests and potentials that you never would have supposed. It's like looking through a tiny straw today; you can only see a fraction of your potential, talents and gifts; your perception of what is possible is very limited. But, over time as you utilize the LifeBalance System, your view will expand, from a tiny hole to a glorious wide perspective where the sky's the limit.

This discovery process reminds me of that played out in the book *Jonathan Livingston Seagull*. The main character, Jonathan, is a seagull who desires to develop his flying abilities beyond that of other gulls. While others are content to expend minimal energy, flying only to obtain food, Jonathan pushes his mind and body, culminating in what he envisions as the ultimate skill level. Upon reaching his ideal however, he suddenly breaks through into a whole new reality, one where he can see possibilities he never imagined. From that point forward, he learns that for those who have eyes to see, life is a series of breakthroughs where we reach our ideal, only to discover a whole new world of growth and progress. It's like climbing a series of mountains: You climb to what you believe is the highest peak and when you reach the top, you suddenly see an even higher mountain off in the distance. With this never-ending-progression picture in mind, you're ready to begin your journey of discovery.

Now it's Your Turn

Exercise:

Imagine you have just won the $20 million lottery. Making money is no longer your concern. After you've purchased your dream home, acquired all the toys and taken all the trips, describe in detail how you would spend your time, talents and resources.

Keep the detailed response from this exercise in your *LifeBalance Workbook*. At the appropriate time, you will learn how to incorporate these things into your *LifeCreed* and work toward making them a reality.

7

How to Begin Your Feelings Journal™

Getting in touch with your deepest feelings
The male vs. female brain

One of the primary benefits of Feelings Journaling is that it will help you prepare to put together what will likely become for you, the most important document in the world: your LifeCreed—the written visualization of your ideal self and your ideal life. The first step in discovering a vision of your ideal self and ideal life is to get in touch or in tune with your deepest feelings. Men generally have a more difficult time doing this than women. Why?

The *typical* male brain is wired very differently than the *typical* female brain. One of the primary differences is in what is known as the Corpus Callosum—a bundle of connections (think of a bundle of electrical wires) linking the left and right hemispheres of the brain. Autopsies have shown that in the typical female brain, the Corpus Callosum has three to four times more connections than the typical male brain. This allows women to be in tune and connected with a greater variety of emotions and feelings at any given time. This also accounts for a woman's ability to intuit and sense things going on around her at a much higher level than most men; she is using significant amounts of both hemispheres of her brain and simply takes in more information at any one time. In addition, as a brain chemical, estrogen takes an already diverse, multi-tasking, "web-thinking" female brain and causes it to diffuse even further.

The male brain, on the other hand, tends to be more narrowing and specialized. Men have a great ability to focus narrowly on a task or goal and block out all superfluous information until the end result is achieved. As a brain chemical, testosterone takes an already narrowing male brain and causes it to narrow even further. During sporting events, physical intimacy, road-rage, etc., large amounts of testosterone are released into the male brain and the male narrowing phenomenon is readily apparent. Because of this tendency to narrow and block out information, men typically have a harder time accessing and expressing "right brain" emotions and feelings. Emotions and feelings stored in the mind-brain are typically accessed in the right hemisphere of the brain, while verbal skills occupy the left hemisphere. Because men typically have fewer connections between the two hemispheres, and tend to narrowly use one specific part of one hemisphere or the other, it is often difficult for men to access and express their feelings, either vocally or in writing. Because men often narrowly focus on the task at hand, they may not notice other things going on around them. This can be frustrating for women, who wonder: "Why can't he see what's going on?" "Doesn't he get it?" "He just doesn't care!" Most men have to work to develop the kind of intuition and wide perspective that comes so easily and naturally to most women.

In men vs. women, one is not better than the other, they are just different and, as a team extremely complimentary. The purpose in describing the differences is to let you know that men most often find it difficult mastering the process of Feelings Journaling. Some women, of course, struggle as well. The key is to just be patient and know that with time and practice you will open more neural passageways into the right side of your brain and develop the ability to uncover, understand and express your feelings better.

Whatever your gender, the Feelings Journal is a powerful tool to help you access and express in writing your deepest feelings. It will take you to places within yourself that you have probably not visited recently—or perhaps ever. Here are some guidelines to help you get started.

A. **Be completely open, honest and unrestricted:** Write whatever you are feeling—positive or negative. Be totally honest and unrestricted. Don't worry about spelling, grammar or sentence structure—just let it flow onto the paper or computer screen, uninterrupted. You can feel completely at ease writing this way because your Feelings Journal is for your eyes only.

B. **For Your Eyes Only**: Your Feelings Journal is for your eyes only. If you have the slightest suspicion that someone could somehow get hold of your journal and read it, you will probably not allow yourself to write it in a completely open, honest and uncensored manner. Don't allow anyone to have access to your Feelings Journal without your permission. Develop appropriate security measures so you will feel more at ease. If you keep a hand-written journal, **do not** use a bound book. Keep your journal in a 3-ring binder so you can add pages as needed or take out and destroy negative entries as described below.

C. Get rid of negative feelings about people, places or things: Your Feelings Journal is an amazing tool for bringing negative feelings you have toward certain people, places or events to the surface, the Privileged Place, and getting rid of them. These can include unresolved issues or traumatic memories you've carried bottled up inside you, even from childhood. Such issues and memories are things you don't want to keep in your journal for future reference. To get rid of these negative feelings about people, places or events, Marriage and Family Counselor, Gary Lundberg, recommends the following 10 Steps:

1. Give yourself permission to be completely free and open in your writing, holding nothing back—no words or descriptions are prohibited—just get it on the paper.

2. Have two pens (no pencils), a large amount of paper, and unlimited time.

3. Go to a quiet place where you can be undisturbed and uninter-rupted—no cell phone allowed!

4. Never direct your writing toward yourself, such as, "I'm such a stupid _____." "I really messed up when I _____." Don't include any direct references, accusations or statements about yourself when expressing your negative feelings.

5. Write about a person or situation associated with a lot of negative emotions.

6. Address the person however you feel about them: "Dear
   _____," or "You dirty, no good _____."

7. Write as fast as you can and don't worry about handwriting,
   spelling, grammar, punctuation, language or flow of thoughts.
   Just let it all gush out onto the paper.

8. If you're in the middle of writing something and a new
   thought or feeling comes, start writing about that—write with
   total abandon.

9. Write until one of three things happens:

   • You become so emotional you must stop yourself.

   • You run out of things to write.

   • You run out of time (hopefully not this one).

10. When one of these three things happens, take all the pages
    you've written and fold and seal them in an envelope. Immedi-
    ately, go to a location (fireplace, incinerator, or even a freshly
    dug hole in the ground) where you can safely burn the enve-
    lope containing all the pages.

Important: Never re-read a single written word. Simply set
fire to the envelope. Imagine the powerful meaning this has as
you see the negative words, feelings, and memories consumed
by the flames, and the ashes float up into the air and disappear.
Many of my clients have described the feeling of a great burden
being lifted from their shoulders. With the words destroyed, no
one will ever read them again, not even you.

One client had recently experienced a bitter divorce. He was filled with anger and resentment and these feelings were negatively impacting every aspect of his life. Incredibly, he Feelings Journaled 142 pages! It required journaling on separate days to get it all out. He took a large wooden toy sailboat, cut off the top and filled it with all 142 pages. Setting the boat on fire, he floated it out onto a lake near his home. He watched the pages and the boat burn and eventually sink out of sight. He said the burden lifted from him that day was nothing short of miraculous. He was able to resume his life, free of the destructive feelings and debilitative emotions.

D. **Develop your skills over time**: Feelings Journaling does not come easily or naturally to most people—especially men. In the beginning it can be difficult, but with practice and time, you'll become progressively more comfortable and skilled at it. It's not unlike learning to play the piano or some other musical instrument: at first your fingers feel awkward and uncoordinated, but in time you begin playing beautiful music. Be patient, start out slowly, only 5–10 minutes a day, and build up from there. You should use your *Feelings Journal Checklist* (Chapter 8) to stimulate thoughts about what you should write. Stick with it, and Feelings Journaling will become one of the most powerful and fulfilling daily activities in your life.

E. **Same Place/Same Time**: The quality of your life today is a direct result of the habits you have formed over time. The key is to form specific habits that lead to the fulfillment of what you want most in life. Developing a daily Feelings Journaling routine is one of the most important habits you can acquire. To do this, set a regular time (preferably first thing in the morning, before everyone is up) and a quiet, private place where you can look out the window, ponder, think and record whatever is on your mind. Doing this at the same time and place every day will quickly establish a new mental model and then a habit.

Some people have a tough time finding peace and quiet at home for Feelings Journaling. LifeBalance clients have used a variety of approaches to remedy this problem. Some pull into a parking lot on the way to work and journal. Others stop by a coffee shop and sit in their "usual spot." And some simply close their office door and take a few minutes to Feelings Journal before starting their work day.

Key: Feelings Journaling will become an appointment with the most important person in your life—you! If you "try to find the time," you'll likely never do it. Make this appointment a major priority in your life. The remarkable benefits in every aspect of your life will amaze you.

Exercise:

If you haven't already done so, take the *Feelings Journal Challenge*: Take 5 minutes each morning and write your feelings. Do it for six of the next seven days. You'll see the difference.

8

Your Feelings Journal™ Checklist

When first beginning the journaling process, many clients complain that, "I just can't think of anything to write." To help you overcome this obstacle, develop a *Feelings Journal Checklist*. As you sit down to Feelings Journal and review this list, certain items will ignite feelings within you and start you writing. To construct your first checklist, make a list of the things in your life you are most concerned about, most desirous to achieve, or most grateful for. You may want to start with the Six Key Relationships in your life (Chapter 3), creating a checklist something like this:

Spiritual

How is my relationship with God?

What can I do to improve it?

Is there a recent—or not so recent—spiritual experience I should record?

Emotional

What am I feeling today? Why?

What is really important in my life? Why?

Where am I improving in my life?

What area in my life needs more attention? Why?

What am I most excited about? Why?

What am I most discouraged about? Why?

Physical

How do I feel physically? What can I do to improve?

What is most discouraging about my physical condition? Why?

How is my diet? What can I do to improve it? How would this benefit me?

How do I feel about my fitness level and exercise? What can I do to improve? How would this make a difference in my life?

Family

How has _____ (name of spouse) blessed my life?

What are _____'s (name of spouse) strengths?

What areas of concern, complaints or disappointments do I have? How have each of my children blessed my life? (List each child separately.)

What are each of their strengths?

What complaints or disappointments do I have?

Are there any areas of concern I should focus on?

Social

How can I improve my interaction with people?

Which of my friends needs some special attention? Why? What can I do to help?

Financial

What am I working toward in my career? Why?

What am I most concerned about? Why?

What do I find most exciting about my work? Why is this exciting?

What do I find most discouraging? Why?

Make Your Own Custom Checklist

The above are just a sample of some of the questions that could be on your checklist. Make your own list according to what's going on in your life. Put any topic that you need to explore your feelings about, such as a specific person, task, goal, talent or concern. Add new items at any time and remove others when you have exhausted all thoughts about the topic. After you create your *LifeCreed*, you may choose to add items from it to your checklist. Obviously, you don't write about every item on the checklist at once. Place the checklist next to your keyboard or writing pad to stimulate your feelings and help you start writing.

Every Day Isn't a Party

Not every day feels like a party. There may be days when the burden seems heavy. Before you begin to Feelings Journal on those mornings, you may find it helpful to flip back a few pages and read something you have written previously. If I could give you one gift, this would be it: The experience of hearing yourself speak about your family, relationships, dreams and aspirations will lift you like nothing else can. When you read your Feelings Journal, you're not reading someone else's words; they are your words, and more importantly your thoughts and feelings. Through the power of the written images you have captured, you will be able to experience these feelings again, when you need them most. It's like fireflies in a bottle.

Now It's Your Turn

Exercise:

Take the *Feelings Journal Checklist* from this chapter and add your own unique elements to it. Then, if you have not already begun doing so, take at least 5 minutes each morning and write your feelings. Use the Checklist as needed. Feelings Journal for six of the next seven days and you'll see results!

Exercise:

Feelings Journal on one of three categories below. Your responses will be used to build the foundation for your first *LifeCreed Statement* in Chapter 11. The three categories have been randomly selected as examples to help you build a basic understanding of the LifeCreed Statement. The three categories match up to the step-by-step instructional process you will go through in Chapter 11.

Using a blank sheet of paper from your LifeBalance Workbook, choose **one** of the following areas and journal your feelings, thoughts and insights by answering the questions as completely and expansively as possible.

Choose <u>one</u> of the following

Spiritual:

Is there anything I can do more spiritual? Why do I want to be more spiritual

Family:

What in my family life would I like to change? If this were changed, how would my family life be different?

Physical:

What part of my diet would I like to change? Why?

9

The 10 Benefits of Your Feelings Journal™

~

You have been taught since childhood to keep a lid on your emotions and assume an outward appearance of composure and control. In a high-tech society of e-mail and tele-conferencing, this tendency toward holding in emotions has become even more entrenched. The business world is fast becoming a cold and sterile environment where feelings are rarely communicated and shared at any significant level. In this high-tech, low-touch world, feelings get buried deeper and deeper, making Feelings Journaling more important than ever.

You may be thinking, "Exactly how will a Feelings Journal benefit me.?" Writing in your Feelings Journal will reward you in 10 powerful ways.

1. **Enter The Privileged Place**: Old dominant mental models and negative habits can only be worked on and eliminated when you bring the process above the surface to the conscious level or *Priv-*

73

ileged Place. Likewise, you can only build new mental models and positive habits in the Privileged Place. In the stress and busyness of life, the tendency is to react automatically and unconsciously according to your dominant habits.

Through your Feelings Journal, you can bring everything you want to ponder, change, develop, prepare for, or accomplish into the Privileged Place where you can do something with it, something about it. Your Feelings Journal is a simple tool you can use every day to bring yourself out of your automatic thought patterns, behaviors and habits, and into the Privileged Place—a place of real power. The Feelings Journal is one of the most effective self-accountability tools you will ever use, making you consciously aware of and responsible for every aspect of your life. It also reminds you to give others permission to hold you accountable.

2. **Capture *Privileged Place Moments***: Can you remember special times in your life when you felt overwhelmed by the emotions, feelings or spirit of the experience? Perhaps it was your wedding day, the birth of your first child, an incredible family vacation, a tender moment with your spouse or a child, the death of a loved one, an inspiring sermon. There are many moments like these when your perspective is clear; the feelings of your heart are rich and deep. These experiences are precious treasures. It is during these times that you dwell in the highest level of the Privileged Place. Sadly, many of these special moments dim over time until they become a faint memory.

The Funeral

Recently I attended the funeral of an extended family member. Among the attendees I noticed her ex-husband from whom she had been divorced for many years. He was a crusty old trucker, very macho in appearance and demeanor, and as expected, showing no emotion. But then, as they were preparing to close the casket, I noticed his expression began to soften. He looked upon her for the last time and then turned his gaze toward his son and grandchildren. Tears began running down his cheeks. I thought to myself, "He's in the Privileged Place!" "What is he thinking about?" I wondered. Perhaps he was wishing he had worked things out and avoided the divorce all those years ago. Maybe he was thinking he should have spent more time with her. Perhaps he was observing his son and remembering all the times he wasn't there for him. And very likely, he was tenderly considering the sweet faces of his young grandchildren and making a commitment that he would not allow any more precious time and opportunities to be lost.

As the funeral ended, I watched him get into his big rig, the tears gone, his face expressionless, and drive away. I knew that most likely within a few days, back on the road, back in his old environment, habits and mindset, his Privileged Place experience would begin to fade, eventually leaving only a faint memory. Gone would be his clarity, his regret, his determination and inner commitment to make a change.

How often have you had special moments when you have been tapped into clarity, inspiration and things spiritual, and then you let them slip away? Don't allow this to happen ever again. The information you receive in these moments can't be found in any self-improvement book, audio program or seminar. You, your situation, and your needs are unique. Through *privileged place moments* you will find answers for you and your family. When they come to you, you must have a way to capture and hold onto to them, so you can revisit, ponder, nurture and develop these answers over time. Don't let these sacred moments slip away— they have great power to relieve your stress and concerns, improve your relationships, and bring you the success and happiness you're searching for.

Keep a Privileged Place Moments Notepad

Keep a small pad of paper with you (or use your PDA) and when you find yourself in the midst of one of these sacred experiences, make a note about your feelings as soon as possible. That evening, or the next morning, review your notes and then Feelings Journal about the experience in detail. When you're feeling down or in need of inspiration, or require a push to recommit to promises you've made to yourself and others, you can go back and relive these experiences as you read your Feelings Journal entries. You can also make a note in your *LifeBalance Workbook* of ideas for additional goals for your *LifeCreed.* You can reference these notes when you are ready to create and record your LifeCreed. Through your LifeCreed you can take your insights from these special *privileged place moments* and start doing something about them on a daily basis.

When something extra special pops above the surface into the Privileged Place, capture it with your Feelings Journal. These treasures are too valuable to lose. Feelings Journaling allows us to bring these experiences, and the emotional images they contain, into our minds on demand. This will be a powerful component in creating a LifeCreed with the potential to change your life. It's an amazing process.

3. **Crystallize Your Thoughts to Work Through Problems**: Have you ever been burdened with a problem, challenge or worry that you can't find a solution to, one you can't get out of your head? Are their times when you feel stressed out, angry, depressed or anxious? On occasion, is your mind overwhelmed with thoughts and activity, so much so that you can't concentrate? You may even have trouble sleeping. Feelings Journaling can help you resolve these situations.

    One client writes, "Whenever I'm confronted with any challenge, problem or emotion I can't work out I immediately go and Feelings Journal. By the time I'm done journaling I find that one of two things has happened. I have the solution or I realize that what was weighing me down is no big deal. Either way, I'm free of the problem or burden and I feel peace. Instead of obsessing and laboring over it like I used to, I can journal and then move on. The amazing thing to me is that my Feelings Journal is always available to me, any time and any place. All I need is a pen and something to write on. Who would've thought something so powerful could be so simple?"

4. **Purge Negative Feelings**: Via your Feelings Journal you can uncover and expel negative thoughts, feelings and memories that have been festering inside you for years. For reasons science is

77

only just discovering, when you take the time to write out worries, negative thoughts and emotions, they begin to lose their power over you. As negativity loosens its choke-hold on you, you are able to see objectively and discard the concerns that drag you down, focusing instead on the positive. With this baggage cleared out, your health, success, attitudes, energy and relationships substantially improve. When new problems and negative thoughts arise, Feelings Journaling will help you resolve them and move on.

Sometimes life can become overwhelming, your mind like a glass filled to capacity and spilling over. Feelings Journaling allows you to clear out your mind and make room for other things. Think of this process like reformatting a computer hard drive. Over time, software conflicts develop, data becomes corrupted, and the drive fills up. After clearing it out, performance increases dramatically.

A client tells of the power of Feelings Journaling in assisting him in getting rid of dark childhood memories:

"I had a really traumatic childhood filled with emotional and physical abuse. I carried a lot of this baggage into my adult life and it was causing problems in my marriage and my relationships with my kids. I learned how to journal my feelings. One Saturday afternoon I spent several hours getting it all out, all the dark, terrible memories, all the anger, all the fear and shame. I held nothing back, not even profanity. My writing took up many pages. When I was finally done I took all the pages and sealed them in an envelope. I took the envelope into my backyard and I lit it on fire. I stood and watched the pages burn and the smoke rise up

into the air and disappear. I can't explain it, but as that smoke floated up I felt a huge burden lift off of my mind and my shoulders. When all that was left were ashes I felt a deep sense of peace. That experience put me on a path to amazing accomplishments in my career, my marriage and my family life."

5. **Prepare to Communicate**: By crystallizing your thoughts and working through any negatives, journaling lets you uncover your feelings for the people you care about. This advance preparation allows for far more healthy and open communication. In addition, Feelings Journaling can help you prepare for important meetings, presentations and speeches. Consider the following examples:

    *   You've had an argument with your spouse and you're still angry. As you journal your angry feelings, you gain perspective on the situation and your anger fades away. You perhaps begin to see where you were at fault. In effect, "yelling" at your spouse on the pages feels almost as good as doing it in person—and then it's out of your system and gone. (Following the 10 steps for getting rid of negative feelings is very helpful.) As you Feelings Journal you talk about how and what you can say to reconcile with your spouse. Later when you discuss the matter with your spouse you find to your amazement that you're able to speak clearly and calmly, your words unfolding exactly as you journaled beforehand.

    *   A very successful client had an important business presentation he needed to make to his partners. Nervous and not sure how to put the presentation together, he put himself in the place of his partners and journaled about their concerns,

feelings and desired outcomes. This exercise crystallized his thoughts and showed him exactly how to structure the information he wanted to communicate. After the presentation his partners commented about how incredibly well prepared he was and how he hit their key points right on the mark.

- You have an interview scheduled with one of your employees and are not sure what to say. You decide to journal about all the talents, qualities and positives this employee demonstrates. During the interview you express appreciation and praise for all of these things. When you have a few suggestions for improvement, they are extremely well received by the employee and you both leave the interview feeling understood, uplifted and motivated. For weeks afterward you notice your relationship with the employee has greatly improved.

- I know a very successful public speaker who uses the Feelings Journal to prepare for his presentations. He visualizes his audience and then writes about their needs, how he can best serve them, how he feels about them as his brothers and sisters. Based on these things, he sketches an outline of his presentation. He envisions himself making the presentation, sees the smiling faces and nods of approval from his audience, hears their applause at the end and then sees himself interacting and answering their questions afterward. With this vision in mind, he writes about how blessed and fulfilled he feels. He often comments how amazed he is that such a simple exercise could have such a powerfully positive effect on his presentations.

6. **Improve Family Relationships**: It's easy to focus on the negative characteristics and flaws of our spouse, children and others close to us. Over the years this focus leads to the formation of dominant negative mental models, fault-finding, sarcasm, nagging and a drifting apart in our closest relationships. Feelings Journaling is a powerful tool for turning our hearts and minds to focus on the positive attributes, gifts and talents of our loved ones and preventing the negative from poisoning and destroying these relationships.

One client is a dedicated athlete. He keeps himself in top physical condition. Several years ago, in the midst of raising a large family, his wife began to put on weight and get out of shape.

He said, "At first I started thinking negative thoughts whenever I looked at her. Then I found myself making critical comments about her weight and appearance. It really hurt her feelings and became a serious wedge in our relationship. Then I started journaling every morning about why I loved her so much. What was it about her that attracted me when we were first dating? What were her outstanding qualities, talents and gifts? How had she blessed my life and our children's lives? From the very first journaling session I started to feel different. I found that the weight issue was a tiny matter compared to all of the wonderful things about her. After a week or so of journaling it just wasn't a big deal any more. My thoughts and feelings about her turned to total love, appreciation and acceptance."

Another client, John, resisted the idea of journaling feelings. He said, "That's just not my thing." When asked, "John, how

81

much time do you spend telling your wife how you feel about her, like you did when you were first courting?" he responded, "I tell her I love her once in awhile." "How much time do you spend with each of your children affirming their unique gifts and talents and building them up?" I inquired. He admitted not very much. In fact, he never really thought much about it.

Like most guys, after the children starting arriving, John focused on working to provide for his family. He worked hard, and at night, like most men, he looked forward to coming home to escape in front of the TV or to his workshop. He tried to spend time with his kids, but the thought of consciously focusing on affirming their gifts had never crossed his mind. When asked about his wife's unique gifts and talents, he mumbled something about her "being a good cook."

He was encouraged to start Feelings Journaling about each member of his family, their unique talents and gifts, why he loved and appreciated them, how he could help each one and make life better for them. He even started asking his wife and children how he could be a better husband and father. At first they were shocked, but soon they began offering him a few suggestions which he journaled about.

It's been three years since John started on his Feelings Journaling adventure. He is amazed at the thoughts and feelings he is able to express when he is with his children. His wife feels loved and nurtured. Instead of the occasional offhand "I love you," he shares his feelings of admiration, appreciation and love with her because he has been Feelings Journaling about them first.

He observed that a side benefit to all of this that he never would have imagined is how it has improved his productivity as a salesman. In the last three years, he has more than doubled his income and he is able to personally relate to his clients far better than ever before. John observed, "I never knew how much of my life I was missing out on by not being in touch with and expressing my feelings." He is committed to Feelings Journaling for the rest of his life.

7. **Receive Inspiration**: As you Feelings Journal, amazing ideas and insights about all aspects of your life will come to mind, and you'll ask yourself, "Where did that answer come from?" Your Feelings Journal will act as a conduit for continual inspiration and as a written record of that inspiration so it's never forgotten and can be retrieved and acted upon at any time in the future.

I believe there is an energy, a spiritual power all around us. It is there for us to tap into and receive knowledge, guidance and insight from. But, we can only do this when we take time to shut out the noise and distractions of the world and bring ourselves into the Privileged Place. One of the most effective tools you will ever use to accomplish this is your Feelings Journal.

8. **Increase Creativity**: After Feelings Journaling for several months, you will have opened up extensive neural pathways to the right side, the creative side, of your brain. As a result, you will find significant increases in your intuition, not only during your journaling but at many other times during the day and night. This increase will usually be noticed more by men, as women typically possess a ready-made intuition as a result of their unique female

brain structure. Whether you are a man or a woman, you will see increases in your overall insight and creativity.

One client tells of how he was working on an important project and hit an impasse—he just couldn't figure out the solution. While Feelings Journaling "a picture" of the solution came into his mind and he furiously jotted down the details. Remarkably, the problem was solved and he was able to proceed.

9. **Write Your Life Story**: As we look back on our lives, there are so many important experiences, insights, lessons and events, they are far too numerous to count or recall. Some we remember with vivid clarity, others are dim and faded, and many are forgotten altogether. Imagine having a record of your feelings and insights during your engagement, your marriage and honeymoon, the birth of each child, your career experiences, the trials, joys, challenges and triumphs that all are part of your life story. Imagine being able to give excerpts from this record as a gift to your spouse, children, parents, siblings and others at key times in their lives.

One of the most valuable and underutilized treasures is the knowledge and wisdom possessed by preceding generations—people who have been through the school of hard knocks, who have learned valuable lessons and gained Solomon-like wisdom. This precious gift should be shared and passed on to those coming up through the ranks. Yet, many have no method for passing on this legacy other than talking from their memories, which significantly fade with time. And many don't like talking about themselves or aren't very good at telling stories or sharing feelings. Use your Feelings Journal to record the special *privileged place moments* in your life about the people, places and events you really care about. You can also use excerpts from your Feelings Journal to create your own life story or autobiography to pass on to family members.

The Feelings Journal is a simple and easy-to-use tool through which you can reflect on and appreciate your life, mentor your children and grandchildren, and pass on a precious legacy that will benefit generations to come.

One client, Jim, occasionally gives selected journal entries as gifts to family members on special occasions. On his 25th wedding anniversary Jim gave his wife a beautiful leather-bound book containing journal entries from their wedding day, the birth of each of their children, and numerous entries containing expressions of his love, gratitude and admiration for his wife. She will treasure that gift always. When each of his children leave home for college or marriage, He gives them special journal entries from the time of their birth to the present. Think of what this does for each child's self-esteem and the bond of love with their father, as they read about his thoughts and feelings for them!

10. **Build Your LifeCreed**: The LifeCreed is a collection of positive, first-person statements about your ideal self and ideal life. Many people have a difficult time identifying specific aspects of their ideal self and life that they want to put into their initial LifeCreed. Through Feelings Journaling you will be able to create the content for your first LifeCreed. Then as you journal your feelings in the future, you will discover new aspects of your ideal self and ideal life that you want to add to your LifeCreed. In turn, as you listen

to your LifeCreed, you will discover feelings you want to journal about. Thus, the Feelings Journal feeds the LifeCreed and the LifeCreed feeds the Feelings Journal—like two interlocking, rotating circles.

For example: Imagine you've been working on a specific goal for some time but you don't seem to be making any real progress. While journaling your feelings about this you suddenly realize you don't want that outcome at all, but something entirely different. You journal about what you really want, why you want it and the steps you must take to achieve it. You add this to your LifeCreed and immediately feel renewed enthusiasm and energy as you begin pursuing your new goal.

What clients say about Feelings Journaling

Over the years, thousands of clients have received incredible benefits in every aspect of their lives as a result of Feelings Journaling. Consider some insights from just one:

"I love to journal because it frees my mind from the information that bombards me from different directions. I receive so much information that I need to take a step back and reflect on what information is important to me so I can live a fulfilled life. I write in my journal to express my views and organize my thoughts. Writing about my feelings helps me to focus on the goals that are important to me and my family. Also, journaling helps me to sort out my problems. I feel that journaling is talking to my best friend, which is ME."

"I am much more creative since I started to keep a Feelings Journal. Journaling challenges my brain to write something each day that is meaningful. It was difficult to write one page a day when I first started.

86

After one year, I don't have any problem writing one page. My goal is to write two pages per day if time permits. Writing the extra page forces my mind to be creative and it forces me to delve into my feelings about the topic I have chosen to write for the day's entry. As a result, I am developing the creative right side of my brain."

"After I journal I find my brain is thinking about what I wrote as I go through the day. My brain, unconscious to me, is thinking about solutions to problems or mulling my feelings so I can come to some conclusion when I'm least expecting it. I find thoughts coming to my mind about problems I wrote about a month ago that just seem to pop into my mind at the appropriate time."

"I have discovered that the words will flow effortlessly from my mouth if I journal about my feelings. For example, I journaled about returning to my former profession a couple of weeks before I had an interview for a position. I wrote my thoughts about the job and my feelings about how I would approach the job. At the interview I thought I had not prepared for it very well. However, the words flowed effortlessly from my mouth and it was one of the best interviews I have ever had. Journaling helped me to prepare for the interview, because I was able to sort my feelings about the job, before I went to the interview."

"Journaling has improved my spiritual life. I write about my feelings about my faith in God and Jesus Christ. Writing about God increases my faith because I am imprinting my thoughts in my mind as I write them on paper. I write about Bible passages that really affect me and these thoughts will come to my mind at the right time when I'm faced with a situation that calls for God's guidance."

"Writing in my Feelings Journal forces my mind to think differently than when I talk. I am able to remain more focused on what I want to accomplish today than I was one year ago because of writing my

87

feelings in my journal. I am always happier and my day feels more fulfilled when I make time to journal because I am taking time away from my busy life to be with myself. As a result, I am better at discovering who I am and identifying what is really important to me."

Now It's Your Turn

Exercise:

By now you should be practicing basic Feelings Journaling every day. You are ready to begin using your Feelings Journal in more advanced and creative ways. Each day, choose one of the **Ten Benefits** categories in this chapter, and directly apply Feelings Journaling to your life as described. You'll be amazed at the results!

Listening to my LifeCreed tape daily helps me to focus on a future I want to have, rather than on a past which no longer applies. In other words, my LifeCreed has "reprogrammed" my world-view which in turn has profoundly affected my actions and behaviors and the quality of my life.

—F. Johnson

10

Tool #2: Your LifeCreed™ Harness the Power of Your Built-In Successability

Aclient and friend shared this story recently:

"Many years ago I heard a song. One lyric in particular has stayed with me through the years: **He carried in his heart a picture of the man that he knew he would become.** *Even before the LifeBalance System, this lyric had significant meaning for me. I knew there was a powerful concept here. Finding the LifeBalance System and the LifeCreed provided the practical implementation for this concept that felt so right. I have been able to clearly define the picture of who I will become, and daily I am making progress towards becoming him."*

It is the purpose of the LifeCreed to define this picture, and then to make it a reality. Consider the LifeCreed as a goal with power. The term 'goal' has become so diluted in our culture, that it has lost most of its ability to motivate and change us. If you're like most, your goals may be ambiguous and weak. You may create New Year's resolutions, and then throw them away before the year has really begun. This inability to motivate ourselves towards accomplishing meaningful goals lies at the heart of the failure of most self-improvement principles. A good idea doesn't make a goal. A desire isn't even enough, and a wish definitely won't get the job done. The process we begin now will define real, powerful, meaningful goals, also known as *Consciously Directed Goals*, and teach you how to implement a simple tool to bring them to pass.

As Napoleon Hill developed his conclusions, the one attribute of successful people that stood out was the fact that each of these people had reduced their major goals to writing—known as their "definite major purpose"—and they reflected on it often. The LifeCreed, an even more powerful tool, will do far greater things for you than the "definite major purpose" did for the people Napoleon Hill researched.

All that you have learned thus far has been leading you to this, the most powerful habit formation and success tool of all: Your *LifeCreed.*

In Chapter 4, you learned about the mind-brain science of success, mental model and habit formation and why people find it so difficult to change. You discovered that you have a natural built-in Successability that you have been using since the day you were born. You learned that in the Privileged Place, you can harness and direct this natural power for the formation of positive, productive mental models and habits, and eliminate negative behaviors. You can now move forward with the confidence that you possess all of the capabilities necessary to accomplish anything you truly desire. Your task now is to learn how to consciously direct your natural Successability. The LifeCreed uses the principles defined in the Three Simple Rules to allow you to accomplish this.

Rule #1: Clearly state your goal and motive in a way that accesses *mental models* with powerful *meaning*.

In order to attach your goals to mental models with powerful meaning, they must contain four key elements:

- State each goal clearly and completely. Keep asking yourself, "What do I mean by that?"

- Clearly state your motive—*why* you want to achieve each goal.

- Visualize yourself already having achieved the goal ("act as if"), and then describe in detail how you feel.

- State your goal in the present tense, creating a powerful expectation.

- Attach a *hook* to your goal and motive. A *hook* is the *how* and *when* you will achieve your goal.

Rule #2: Engage in Daily Practice and Repetition in the Privileged Place.

Your dominant mental models and habits have been created, accessed and expanded over many years of daily practice and repetition. You must find a way to duplicate the same type of daily practice and repetition.

Rule #3: Give Yourself and Others Permission to Hold You Accountable.

In the buzz of everyday life it's easy to lose awareness of your goals and slip below the surface, back into your old habits You need to employ a system that gives you and special people in your life the permission and the tools to remind you and hold you accountable.

An Easy Daily Method for Applying the *Three Simple Rules*

We all live in the real world; a world filled with appointments, obligations, making a living, family responsibilities, pressures and stress. It's easy to get distracted, caught up in the busyness of everyday life, or just stuck in the same old rut. It's impossible to constantly stop, consciously bring each important goal into our mind, and then apply the Three Simple Rules. But what if all you had to do to fully implement the Three Simple Rules for every goal you desire is put in a CD or cassette tape and listen? Once you create and record your own custom LifeCreed, it will be that simple.

Your LifeCreed is a written and recorded visualization of the ideal person you want to be and the ideal life you want to live in each of the six key relationships or areas of your life: Spiritual, Emotional/ Intellectual, Physical, Family, Social and Financial. As you listen to your LifeCreed daily, you bring each of your goals into the Privileged Place where you can create the new mental models and habits necessary to make those goals a reality.

Consider how your LifeCreed directs your mind-brain's natural habit-forming processes, or *Successability*, to attain the things you want most in life:

- **Self-Talk**: Over your lifetime the voice you hear the most is your own. This is the voice that is most familiar to you. It is also the voice that you consider to be the most credible—you believe your own voice more than anyone else's. This is why what you say to yourself is so critical! Studies show that your self-talk dramatically increases mental force and the activation of specific mental models in your mind-brain. Every day people reinforce and perpetuate negative mental models and habits through their negative self-talk.

Through your LifeCreed you will use powerfully positive self-talk to generate amazing results in your life. In addition, you will record your LifeCreed when you are feeling especially good about yourself and positive about life. These emotions will be reflected in your voice as you record your LifeCreed. Then in the future, if you're having a down day, you can listen to your LifeCreed in your positive, optimistic voice and get an instant pick-me-up. This powerful self-talk in your LifeCreed generates tremendous mental force that can be used toward the formation of new mental models and habits and the attainment of your goals.

- **Expectation**: Your LifeCreed is recorded in your own voice; states each goal in the present tense—as if it is already coming to fruition; states your motive and how you feel having attained your goal. These elements combined communicate a powerful *expectation* to your mind-brain. In the proper setting, and with powerful meaning, your mind-brain cannot distinguish between what is real and what is hoped for.

   Over time, you build mental models that become dominant and your mind-brain begins responding as if what you desire is already a reality. As you listen to your LifeCreed on a daily basis, many of your goals and dreams will begin to unfold right before your eyes. You get what you expect. You attract what you think about most.

In addition, you also state every goal or ideal in the first-person. This directs you to take responsibility for your own future. You should never force or rely on others to make your dreams come true. You need to direct your own life and strive to lead and influence others to achieve greatness in their lives.

- **Accelerated-Learning Music**: Have you ever noticed how much more powerful a movie is if the soundtrack is really well done? It seems to be a more emotional experience, and everything else about the movie seems more powerful. Think of *Accelerated-Learning Music* as the soundtrack to your LifeCreed. Music has the ability to jump right to the emotional areas of our mind, and our LifeCreed is carried along.

  You will record your LifeCreed with specific accelerated-learning music playing in the background. As reported in Ostrander and Schrader's book *Super Learning*, scientists in the former Soviet Bloc were first to make the startling discovery that a certain kind of music can put the mind-brain into an accelerated-learning state. Since that time, extensive research has clearly shown that the larghetto or andante movements in Baroque concertos, a restful tempo of about 60 beats per minute, actually open up pathways and connections throughout the mind-brain, accelerating the formation and expansion of mental models. Baroque composers typically scored this peaceful, soothing music for string instruments. Accelerated-Learning Music super-charges your LifeCreed and your results. (There is a CD in the back of this book which contains Accelerated-Learning Music selections.)

94

- **Visualization**: As you listen to your LifeCreed, images of your ideal self and ideal life will appear on the stage of your mind—as if it's already a reality. Because your LifeCreed is in your own voice, contains elements of powerful meaning and is accompanied by Accelerated-Learning Music, you don't have to consciously force this visualization—it comes very naturally to your mind-brain. It's like seeing a movie of your ideal future that triggers powerful feelings and emotions. These previews of your ideal future provide yet another source for building desired mental models and generating the mental force to activate those mental models in fulfilling all that is stated in your LifeCreed.

  In addition, while listening to your LifeCreed, ideas, impressions, new goals and desires will come into your mind. Keep a small tape recorder or pen and pad near so you can make note of these things. Later, you can Feelings Journal about them and at your discretion, add them to your LifeCreed.

- **New Mental Models**: With all of the components of your Life-Creed combined, you will have one of the most powerful life-changing tools at the push of a button everyday. As you listen to your LifeCreed, you will begin forming new mental models with powerful meaning. After a short period of time, these will begin overriding and replacing old mental models. You will notice changes in your thinking, attitudes, emotions and outlook on life—you will be thinking differently and *you attract what you think about*. Relationships will begin improving, stress diminishing, and your success increasing.

As you develop new mental models, your physiology will begin to change. In situations where you were normally stressed, you are calmer; where you have felt anger, you feel more peaceful; where there has been fear, you begin moving forward with more confidence. You are teaching your mind-brain to respond in new, more positive, healthful and productive ways.

Just as advertisers design their commercials to activate powerful mental models and emotions in your mind-brain, causing you to respond in a specific way, likewise, your LifeCreed will be your own custom "advertisement" in moving you toward the future you desire.

- **Daily Practice and Repetition**: One of the weaknesses of virtually every self-improvement system lies in the fact that they are too tedious, complex or ambiguous to create the consistent practice and repetition required over time. Most people give up and return to their old ways before new mental models and new habits can be formed. One of the reasons the LifeCreed produces such amazing results—when so many other programs fail—is that it's easy to implement on a daily basis. You simply turn on your tape player or insert your CD and start listening. These listening sessions comprise the consistent repetition that is so critical to creating new habits and lasting success. In your LifeCreed, you have a dynamically evolving lifetime vehicle to which you can attach any new insights, ideas, thoughts or goals and make them a permanent part of your life.

By creating a Creed and listening to it, I have actually changed my life with relative ease. Positive expectation is used in the LifeBalance program as a secret weapon against negative thoughts and the resulting actions. —G. R. Swiss

11

Creating Your First LifeCreed™ Statement

The LifeCreed is the most exciting personal growth tool ever developed. Beginning with just a few specific goals, your LifeCreed will grow to encompass all of your *Six Key Relationships*. Feelings Journaling will help you identify your goals or the specific details of your ideal self and ideal life. Turning your goals and ideals into *LifeCreed Statements* is the first step in turning the picture of who you want to become into the reality of who you are.

Don't get bogged down in trying to make your LifeCreed perfect the first time. Keep in mind two very important points as you begin the creation process for your initial LifeCreed:

1. **This is only the beginning**: The purpose of your LifeCreed is to act as a catalyst and a source of inspiration to get your discovery process started. Daily, as you listen to your LifeCreed and write

97

in your Feelings Journal, a flood of ideas, realizations and desired goals will come into your mind. After two or three weeks you will be ready to revise your initial LifeCreed by adding some of this new information. Remember, your LifeCreed is not static; you don't create it once and that's it. Your LifeCreed is an ever-evolving document. As you discover more about who you truly are and the life you really want, you will continue adding these discoveries to your LifeCreed for a lifetime of increasing success, happiness and fulfillment. Your initial LifeCreed is only the beginning of a life-long refining process.

2. **Get the discovery process moving:** Remember the old steam locomotives you've seen in western movies? From a dead stop, the locomotive strains and groans; the first few chugs turn the wheels, but they slip on the hard steel tracks. With the next few chugs the wheels gain some traction and the train slowly creeps forward, gradually picking up speed until it's sailing smoothly down the tracks.

   The key to discovering and attaining your ideal self and life is to start the journey—get the train moving. Create your initial LifeCreed as quickly as possible and start using it to generate amazing results in your mind-brain and your life. Don't worry that it isn't "good enough," you'll have lots of opportunities to improve it in the future. Just get the train moving!

Create Your First LifeCreed Statement

At the end of Chapter 8, you completed an exercise where you Feelings Journaled in response to questions in one of three categories.

98

Go to your *LifeBalance Workbook* and retrieve your responses to this exercise. Applying a simple *Seven-Step Process*, you will now convert your Feelings Journaling response into a *LifeCreed Statement*.

The Grand Key—Write and Think in the *Present Tense*: To the mind-brain, *meaning* is everything. When meaning is powerful, your mind-brain does not distinguish between what is real and what is imagined—it simply responds. Control meaning and you control your future. (See the *Mind-brain Science Appendix* for more information.)

One of the most effective ways to create powerful meaning in your mind-brain is to express an expectation—to state something as if it already is a reality. Combine this expectation with a statement about why you want it and how you will feel once you've attained it, and you have the most powerful mind-brain meaning imaginable. As your mind-brain forms mental models according to your expectations, you will find your expectations become self-fulfilling prophecies.

For maximum effectiveness, as you create your first LifeCreed Statement, express everything in the *present tense*. Use words such as "I am," "I do," "I deserve," "I am becoming." Avoid "I hope," "I want," "I wish." For more examples of present-tense statements, see the Appendix.

The 7-Step Process

Step #1: Identify your goals.

As you review your Feelings Journal entry from the assignment in Chapter 8, identify and underline any specific goals you want to

LEO WEIDNER & MARK KASTLEMAN

achieve. Take a **new sheet of paper** and write down each goal you have underlined.

Step #2: Dig deeper.

Ask yourself, "What do I mean by that?" Look at each goal or ideal you have underlined and written down. Is the goal clear and defined? If a stranger were reading it, would it be clear enough to really understand? If not, expand the goal by answering the question: "What do I mean by that?" Keep asking this question and expanding the goal until you can go no further. Your mind-brain will not lock onto a goal and link it to a specific mental model with powerful meaning unless the goal is clear and specific. Be sure to write everything in the present tense.

Step #3: Find your motive.

Next to the expanded description of each goal, clearly and simply state "why" you want to achieve it—what is your *motive*? Next, visualize yourself already in possession of your goal and briefly describe how you feel having already attained it. Be careful not to state "I will feel . . ." or "When I have it I feel . . ." See yourself already having attained it and state how you feel right then. Only by stating the feeling in the present tense can you produce the full power of meaning.

Your *motive* or *why* is the real power in a LifeCreed Statement. Remember, you get what you expect. You are reprogramming your expectations, and this takes powerful, emotional motives to accomplish. If you can't identify a powerful motive, then your goal is either not stated clearly enough, or it is not as important as you thought. If you can't define some reason that accomplishing this goal will be exciting to you, you need to dig deeper. Ask, "Why do I want this?" Then, ask it again until you have that emotional response. Be sure your motive is clear.

The most fun part of creating a LifeCreed Statement is imagining how it will feel to have accomplished your goal. When you have a quiet moment, just imagine yourself having already done it. How does it feel? How does your family respond to it? Your friends, colleagues, or other people you respect? Write these feelings down and capture them. It's like fireflies in a bottle.

"If you can imagine it, you can achieve it. If you can dream it, you can become it."

Step #4: Check for negative statements.

It's common in setting goals to state what we "don't want." Look for any phrases that are the least bit negative, such as: "I never want to," "I don't," "I shouldn't." Replace them with a positive: "I always," "I do," "I am committed to," Follow the positive phrase with a statement of what you are doing to create a positive outcome—be proactive! Remember, as you listen to your recorded LifeCreed, your mind-brain will begin responding and your positives will become a reality.

Many traditional self-improvement and therapy programs teach individuals to break negative habits by focusing on avoiding the negative consequences. That is, when you get the urge to act out a particular behavior, you simply remind yourself of all the pain it will cause you, and this motivates you to avoid it. While this works for some people, it is ineffective for many. Think of the millions who smoke, all the while knowing it's killing them. Think back when you were a teenager being lectured by your parents about the myriad negative consequences of a certain behavior. How often did you go and do it anyway? Mind-brain science clearly shows that we are far more motivated by a powerfully positive reward or outcome than avoiding a negative one. Attach powerful motive and meaning to the positive outcome, and your success is virtually guaranteed.

Step #5: Write in the first-person.

Your LifeCreed is your map. Nobody else will be looking at it, so there's no reason for it to contain instructions for anyone else. You cannot control the actions of others or rely on them to make your goals and ideals a reality. Search through your statement and look for any instances where you try to control or direct the actions of others. Change these to the first-person and adjust the wording so that instead it indicates what "I can do." For example: "If only she would . . ." might be changed to "I create an environment where she can . . ." "When my boss . . ." may be changed to "I make it easy for my boss to . . ." Again, be sure to state everything in the present tense.

Step #6: Develop *hooks.*

A hook is the ***how, where*** and ***when*** of a specific goal. If you want to go from Los Angeles to New York City, and you get on the freeway and head *west*, it doesn't matter how strong your desire is, you won't get there. So, while the goal and your motive are incredibly important, the *hook*, the *how, where* and *when* you will do the things you've identified, is essential.

For example: To get to New York, take US 101 North, leave today at 4:00 P.M., in my car.

"I tell my wife I love her" might be better stated "I tell my wife 'I love you' three times each day." "I accomplish my goal in 2006" would be better stated "I accomplish my goal by Tuesday, August 22,

2006." Be careful, however, not to load your LifeCreed with too many *hooks*. Be selective in including action steps and calendared activities.

Step #7: Keep in the present tense.

Check your LifeCreed statements for "leaks." Review the final version of your LifeCreed Statement and look for phrases that are not in the present tense and change them to the present tense. This insures the maximum effectiveness of your LifeCreed.

Note: If you consider the Seven-Step Process, you can summarize it in brief form using a model you are already familiar with: **What, Why, When, Where and How**.

SAMPLES OF THE LIFECREED STATEMENT FORMATTING PROCESS

To provide you with additional help in applying the *Seven-Step Process*, the following examples are provided for each of the three categories from the exercise in Chapter 8. The LifeCreed Statement formatting process is completed for each one:

LifeCreed Statement Formatting Sample #1

This sample follows the Seven-Step Process for someone who Feelings Journaled about the questions in category one: Spiritual.

Spiritual:

Is there anything I can do to make my life more spiritual? Why do I want to be more spiritual? **Feelings Journal entry**: "I need to get closer to God so I can feel more peace in my life."

103

Step #1:   Identify specific goals or ideals I want to achieve

I need to get closer to God

Note: From this point forward, state everything in the present tense.

Step #2:   What do I mean by that?

I need to get closer to God: **I spend more time praying, reading my Bible and being active in my church**.

Step #3:   What is my motive (why) and how do I feel once I've achieved it?

When I pray **I feel God's spirit and I receive his guidance. Feeling this, I know there isn't anything I can't get through or accomplish. It feels wonderful and I am developing amazing confidence and inner peace.** Reading the Bible **brings me closer to God. I feel tremendous peace and strength wash over me as I read the scriptures**. I am committed to being active in my religion. **By worshiping with others I can offer my support and strength and feel of theirs. I love the feeling of giving and serving others and God. This is a wonderful and fulfilling part of my life.**

Step #4:   Change any negative statements to positives

None to change

Step #5:   Change everything to the First-Person

It's already in first-person

Step #6: **What is my hook—action steps (how, where) and timing (when)?**

Every morning and every evening I pray **in the privacy of my den**. As I pray I feel God's spirit and receive his guidance. Feeling this, I know there isn't anything I can't get through or accomplish. It feels wonderful and I am developing amazing confidence and inner peace. **Every morning from 7:00–7:30**, I spend time reading the Bible **in the peace and quiet of my den** and it brings me closer to God. I feel tremendous peace and strength wash over me as I read the scriptures. **Every Sunday from 10:00 A.M. to 12:00 noon**, I attend worship services. By worshiping with others I offer them my support and strength and feel of theirs. I love the feeling of giving and serving others and God. This is a wonderful and fulfilling part of my life.

Step #7: **Review and make sure everything is in present tense**

This is now a completed LifeCreed statement ready for recording!

LifeCreed Statement Formatting
Sample #2

This sample follows the Seven-Step Process for someone who Feelings Journaled about the questions in category two: Family.

Family:

What in my family life would I like to change? If this were changed, how would my family life be different?

105

Feelings Journal Entry:

"I need to show more patience and demonstrate positive attitudes with the kids. I need to make a concerted effort to have at least one meal together as a family per day. Our home would be a happier, more peaceful place to be."

Step #1: Identify specific goals or ideals I want to achieve

<u>I need to show more patience and demonstrate positive attitudes with the kids. I need to make a concerted effort to have at least one meal together as a family per day</u>.

Note: From this point forward, state everything in the present tense.

Step #2: What do I mean by that?

<u>Show more patience and demonstrate positive attitudes with the kids</u>: **I encourage love and understanding in my family by setting an example of patience and a positive attitude with Cindy and the kids.**

<u>Have at least one meal together as a family per day</u>: **We have family dinner together every night.**

Step #3: What is my motive and how will I feel once I've achieved it?

I encourage love and understanding in my family by setting an example of patience and a positive attitude with Cindy and the kids. **I don't like the contention** that is in our home at times. As a result of my good example, **my wife and kids are happy and** our home is a positive and peaceful place for them to be. I love the wonderful feeling that permeates our home.

We have family dinner together every night. **This is our time in our busy lives when we can be together, talk and get closer to each other. I know I'm doing a better job as a father in bringing my family together for this quality time. I love the feelings this realization brings me**.

Step #4: Change any negative statements to positives

I don't like the contention that is in our home at times: **In our home contention is a thing of the past.**

Step #5: Change everything to the first-person

As a result of my good example, my wife and kids are happy and our home is a positive and peaceful place for them to be: **I create an environment** where my wife and kids **can be** happy and our home **can be** a positive and peaceful place for them to be.

We have family dinner together every night: **I am committed to creating an atmosphere** where my family **can enjoy** gathering together for dinner every night.

Step #6: What is my *hook*—action steps (how, where) and timing (when)?

I encourage love and understanding in my family by setting an example of patience and a positive attitude with Cindy and the kids. In our home contention is a thing of the past. **Whenever there is contention, I repeat this phrase in my mind: "I allow**

each member of my family their weaknesses and I look for the good in them and mention this whenever possible."

As a result of my good example, I create an environment where my wife and kids can be happy and our home can be a positive and peaceful place for them to be. I love the wonderful feeling that permeates our home.

I am committed to creating an atmosphere where my family can enjoy gathering together for dinner **every night from 6:00-7:00. During this hour I encourage warm and friendly conversation. I invite family members to share something special from their day. I use this time to express my love and praise. I express my appreciation to each of my children and my wife and mention at least one positive quality they possess.** This is our time in our busy lives when we can be together, talk and get closer to each other. I know I'm doing a better job as a father in bringing my family together for this quality time. I love the feelings this realization brings me.

Step #7: Review and make sure everything is in present tense:

This is a completed *LifeCreed* statement, ready for recording!

LifeCreed Statement Formatting
Sample #3

Physical:

What part of my diet would I like to change? Why?

Feelings Journal Entry:

"I eat way too much junk food. I want to eat healthier, nutritional foods so I can look and feel better.

Step #1: Identify specific goals or ideals I want to achieve

I eat way too much junk food. I want to eat healthier, nutritional foods

Note: From this point forward, state everything in the present tense.

Step #2: What do I mean by that?

Way too much junk food: **All the fried, refined and processed stuff I eat.**

Healthy, nutritional foods: **I eat foods that are as close as possible to the state in which my Creator made them.**

Step #3: What is my motive (why) and how will I feel once I've achieved it?

I avoid all fried, refined and processed foods. I eat foods that are as close as possible to the state in which my Creator made them. **My body is a natural system and I know it thrives on natural foods, not man-made substances. Eating fresh, nutritional foods makes me feel energized, light on my feet and I look radiant and healthy. With my new way of eating, I'm losing weight and I look and feel fabulous! My health is fantastic. When flu or colds come, they just go right past me. I'm on my way to a long and healthy life and I have the great satisfaction**

knowing I'm being responsible and wise in taking care of my body and investing in my future.

Step #4: Change any negative statements to positives

I *avoid* all fried, refined and processed foods: **I only eat** foods that are as close as possible to the state in which my Creator made them. My body is a natural system and I know it thrives on natural foods, not man-made substances.

Step #5: Change everything to the first-person

Everything is already in first-person

Step #6: What is my hook—actions steps (how, where) and timing (when)?

I only eat foods that are as close as possible to the state in which my Creator made them. My body is a natural system and I know it thrives on natural foods. Eating fresh, nutritional foods makes me feel energized, light on my feet and I look radiant and healthy. **Every morning I have fresh fruit for breakfast and the same for a mid-morning snack. For lunch I have a big salad with lots of fresh vegetables. I have some fruit in the afternoon, then for dinner I eat a moderate-size meal of a variety of wholesome foods. In the evening if I want a snack, I eat only fresh fruits and vegetables**. With my new way of eating, I'm losing weight. **By June 1st of this year I've lost 40 pounds**. I look and feel fabulous! My health is fantastic. When flu or colds come, they just go right past me. I'm on my way to a long and healthy life and I have the great satisfaction of knowing I'm being responsible and wise in taking care of my body and investing in my future.

Step #7: Change everything to the present-tense

This is a completed LifeCreed Statement ready for recording!

You now have a basic understanding of how to format a Feelings Journal entry into a LifeCreed Statement—a *Consciously Directed Goal*. You are ready to discover your ideal self and ideal life in each of your six key relationship areas, and create LifeCreed Statements for each. Once you have done this you will have all of the content you need to record your initial LifeCreed. Soon you will begin experiencing the life-changing results of listening to your personal LifeCreed on a daily basis.

Now It's Your Turn

Exercise:

Following the instructions and guidelines in this chapter, complete your first *LifeCreed Statement*.

My first draft of my Creed left me feeling great—like my life had purpose and excitement—I loved listening to it. I'm totally amazed at how many changes I have made in my life seemingly without any effort. Now I'm always thinking of new things to add to my Creed, new things that I want to do, new ways of behaving.

—Alysia

12

Discover Your Ideal Self and Your Ideal Life: Create Your Complete LifeCreed™

Understanding the mechanics of creating LifeCreed statements in the best format to make them effective, now allows us to focus on the exciting aspects of the LifeCreed itself. Like learning to drive a car, there's not much joy in learning all the rules in the drivers handbook, and the first few times out on the road can be incredibly stressful. The real fun begins when we have all the mechanics down and can use our new skills to get somewhere. With the details of correctly formatting your LifeCreed Statements out of the way, let's tap into the real power of your LifeCreed.

The first step in creating your LifeCreed is to begin the process of discovery, uncovering the hopes, dreams, gifts and talents that are the real you; the picture of you that you carry in your heart. You already have begun this process by daily writing in your Feelings Journal. Answering the *LifeCreed questions* will now help you greatly expand this process.

Keep in mind that because of expectations or limitations placed on you by others, or simply as a byproduct of your own doubts, fears or negative thoughts, some aspects of your true identity may have lain dormant or been repressed for many years. Some clients have expressed a feeling of frustration in their first attempt at answering the questions: "I feel like two people: one part of me wants to open up while the other is preventing it." This is a case of the *true identity* fighting to be recognized while the *false identity* wants to remain as is, in its safe little comfort zone. After years of listening to their own self-talk or the comments of others, many clients have trouble giving themselves permission to get in touch with their true self and potential, to think and dream big, to think in terms of their "ideal." It's time for you to begin the process of discovering and freeing your true identity and get in touch with your ideal self and ideal life. A client recently wrote me:

> *"Leo, I began Feelings Journaling several months ago, and had some difficulty moving on to the LifeCreed. As I began the process, I kept stumbling with the concept of my "ideal self." I didn't think I had one. So many years of living my life to please others, and feeling insecure and doubtful about my own abilities, made it hard for me to imagine anything for myself. You asked me what was exciting to me, and so I began to take some time in Journaling to write about it. I couldn't believe what came out. I have dreams and hopes for myself and my family that are still exciting when I read them today. These became the focal point of my first LifeCreed. It was only a few statements, but they mattered very much to me. Every time I listen to my LifeCreed I hear them again, and the same excitement is there."*

LifeCreed Questions

Below are lists of questions that have proven very effective in helping people tap into their true identity, and in this mind set discover

114

their vision of their ideal self and ideal life. In the process you may feel inward pressure to answer the questions in a certain way—how you "should feel" or "ought to feel."—which is derived over the years from parents, spouses, bosses, society, self-talk, etc. Temporarily place these feelings and responses in the "false identity category" and allow yourself the complete freedom to express your true identity.

Important Note: The LifeCreed questions are separated into seven sections to provide simplicity and structure in exploring the various elements of your relationships, ideal self and ideal life. As you begin to put together your initial LifeCreed, please understand it is not intended that your LifeCreed be created in sections. Your LifeCreed content may be stated in whatever order or placement makes sense to you.

For example, if you're setting up a workout schedule to get in better shape, you may choose to put this in your LifeCreed in the spot where you discuss your relationship with your sweetheart. In other words, your motive for getting in shape is how much it will please your mate. You describe how much you love her, how wonderful she is, how she deserves the best, how you want to become a "hunk" for her. This is just one example of how you can mix and match your goals in various locations throughout your LifeCreed, depending on what makes the most sense to you and what will create the most powerful meaning and motive.

You don't have to answer every question. They are presented only as a catalyst to help you unlock your true identity, goals, dreams, gifts and talents. As you review the questions, answer only those that provoke a thought you would like to explore or that trigger powerful feelings. If other ideas and feelings come to you in the process, write them down as well. Use a separate piece of paper for each section. As you answer the questions, write whatever floats into your mind. Be completely truthful and honest, and even negative if necessary. Just get everything you're thinking and feeling down on paper. In essence, this is a *Feelings Journaling* exercise. If something doesn't come to you in an area, skip it. Don't let it hold you up. You don't have to address each area immediately. You may find that these areas provide a starting point for Feelings Journaling in the future. But don't let them bog you down now. It's important to get the most immediate areas down now, and begin the process.

Some questions pertain to your future goals. Answer these questions according to the *ideal* you would like, not what you perceive as realistic or where you are today. Remember, the purpose of the LifeCreed questions is to begin the process of discovering your true identity and your vision of your ideal self and ideal life. Write as freely and openly as you can. Don't worry about structure, grammar or spelling. When you are finished, you will go back and use the Seven-Step Process to convert your entries into LifeCreed Statements. At this point, your only aim is to get your thoughts and feelings on paper, or on your computer screen. Using the *Six Key Relationships* as general categories will get you started.

Spiritual: My relationship with my Creator

- Is there anything I can do to make my life more spiritual? Is so, why do I want to be more spiritual?

- Do I honestly want to become more religious? In what way(s)? Why?

- Should I spend more time reading or listening to religious or spiritual literature? Like what? What would this do for me?

116

- Am I tolerant of others' beliefs? What concerns do I have about my attitude in this area?

- What blessings in life am I most grateful for? Why?

- What kinds of people or events make my inner spirit come alive? Why?

Emotional/Intellectual: My relationship with myself

- What mental strengths would I like to foster in myself? Why?

- What intellectual strengths would I like to nourish? Why?

- What can I do to cultivate a better self-image?

- What behaviors and/or thoughts would I like to change? If these were changed, how would my life be different?

- What books would I like to read? Why?

- What special knowledge or degrees would I like to obtain? Why?

- What are some other personal qualities I would like to promote in myself? Why do I believe these are important?

Physical: My relationship with my body

- How do I feel about the way I look? Why do I feel this way?

- Looking at my physical appearance, the aspects I like most or am most proud of include _____. Why?

- The aspects I like least or am least proud of include _____. Why?

- What are my ideal weight and measurements? Why do I believe these are ideal?

- What elements of an exercise program would I like to include in my daily/weekly routine? (Give details)

- What part of my diet would I like to change? Why?

Family: My relationship with my spouse and children

- What can I do to be a better spouse? How would this improve my marriage?

- I can show my spouse I love him/her by _____. I can do this daily by _____.

- I can show my spouse I want to improve our marriage by _____.

- What positive qualities in my spouse do I want to reinforce?

- How would having a date night with my spouse each week improve my marriage?

- How can I show my spouse how I truly feel?

- I show my spouse I put him/her first, before my work, by _____.

- I express approval to my spouse by _____.

- What things about my family am I proud of? Why do these things make me proud?

- What in my family life would I like to change? If this were changed, how would my family life be different?

- How can I encourage more love in my family?

118

- How much quality time do I spend with my family? How much time, quality and quantity, would I like to spend? What would I do with this time?

- How can I spend twenty minutes a day with each one of my kids?

- I show affection and attention to each family member by _____.

- I can openly and honestly communicate with each family member without being defensive by _____.

- My loved ones can tell me how they feel without fear because I _____.

- I sometimes make my family feel like I put my work first when I _____.

- I can show my family they are more important to me than work by _____.

Social: My relationship with others

- How do I feel when I'm around other people? Why?

- How would I like others to treat me differently? Why?

- What can I do to be more open and free with others?

- What dreams of leadership do I have? Why?

- What can I do to be a better listener? How would this improve my social life?

- Whom do I offend, and why?

- What can I do to find the courage to open up and ask trusted friends for advice on how I can be better?

Financial: My relationship with money and my career

- If I could have the ideal job, what would it be? Why would this be ideal?

- What excites me the most about my present job? Why is this exciting?

- What things about my work would I like to change? Why?

- Do I work too many hours? Why do I do this?

- What one thing could I do to increase my effectiveness at work? How specifically, would this increase my effectiveness?

- How much money would I like to earn each year? What would I do with the extra money? Why am I not making this much now?

General: My relationship to my Overall Life

- Who am I? (This question can stimulate a flood of thoughts.)

- My role in life is to _____. Why do I feel this is my role?

- I would like to be recognized for _____. Why?

- What are my greatest talents/skills/gifts?

- My greatest frustrations about "me" are _____. Why are these things frustrating?

- The habits I would most like to get rid of include _____. How would my life be better if these habits were eliminated?

- The habits I would most like to acquire include _____. How would my life be better if I fostered these habits?

- If I had just won the lottery and money was no longer a concern, what would I do with my time? Why would I spend my time this way?

- The one thing I have always wanted to do is _____. Why?

- Where would I like to travel? What would I do once I got there?

- Ultimately, who do I want to be? Why?

Creating Your First LifeCreed

Just as you did Chapter 11, follow the Seven-Step Process to convert your answers to the LifeCreed questions into LifeCreed Statements. If you're still having trouble with the formatting, **please go to the Appendix and review the *Sample LifeCreeds* section.**

There is no point in simply copying the LifeCreeds of others. Your LifeCreed is unique to you. This is precisely why you should not review the Sample LifeCreeds section until after you have answered the LifeCreed questions and done your best to format your answers into LifeCreed Statements. Use the sample LifeCreeds as a tool for helping you expand and refine your own LifeCreed.

Important: Do not get bogged down in your review of the sample LifeCreeds. Avoid the temptation to compare your LifeCreed Statements to others. Creating a LifeCreed is not a writing contest to see who can produce the most flowery, eloquent statements or the most elaborate or complete LifeCreed. Your LifeCreed is for you and you alone. No one else should ever be allowed to read it. It is the unique expression of your deepest feelings, dreams and ideals.

121

As you review the sample LifeCreeds, don't allow yourself to be sidetracked by the feeling "mine isn't good enough—I need to work on it before I can record it."

Many clients have spent months or even years working on their initial LifeCreed, trying to make it better or perfect before they record it. This violates the very purpose of the LifeCreed. Your LifeCreed is a tool of discovery. As you listen to it each day, you will uncover new insights, ideas, feelings, dreams, gifts, talents and aspirations, and then add these to your ever-evolving LifeCreed. Consider the following experience of one of my clients:

"After weeks of creating, revising, starting over, and over again, I still didn't have a LifeCreed I liked. My wife had picked up some of the materials I received from you, and got very excited. She started Journaling, and working on her LifeCreed. Within a week she had recorded hers! This motivated me to get with it. I sat down and gave it my best shot. I recorded it the next day. I've been listening to it for several weeks and can already see the areas I want to improve. I have to thank you (and my wife for the motivation to get something recorded, and not wait for it to be perfect."

After a while, some parts of your initial LifeCreed might give you *Creed Nausea*—"If I have to listen to that one more time I think I'll throw-up!" When this happens, don't stop listening to your LifeCreed. Simply make a note to change it when you next make revisions. It takes time to filter all the boring parts out of your LifeCreed, so be patient; keep listening and keep Feelings Journaling.

Trying to create the "perfect" LifeCreed is an illusion. You will never do it—it will simply continue to expand and evolve as you do. It is a work in progress, a continuing journey of discovery and achievement that hopefully will never end.

Glean a few ideas from the sample LifeCreeds, make some modifications to your own accordingly, then move on as quickly as possible to the recording of your LifeCreed. The sooner you are listening to your LifeCreed every day, the sooner you will begin seeing the realization of your ideal self and your ideal life.

Additional LifeCreed Content

In addition to your LifeCreed question responses, and insights from the sample LifeCreeds, there are some optional things that you can add to your LifeCreed. Consider the following:

1. **Your LifeBalance Workbook:** You have been using your Life-Balance Workbook to complete exercises at the end of various chapters. Go back and review your Workbook for additional ideas for your LifeCreed Statements. Pay special attention to the exercises you completed in Chapters 5 and 6.

2. **Unique Gifts and Talents You Are Grateful For:** Too often in our hectic lives we don't stop to reflect on the things we're really good at—our own unique gifts and talents. You may have had a much better connection with these gifts and talents when you were a child. Then as a result of career counseling, college majors, the pressures and expectations of others or just getting into the daily routine and grind of life, you likely lost track of these things, or buried them completely.

    What are you great at? What unique gifts and talents has your Creator endowed you with? You may have difficulty identifying these things yourself. Perhaps you should ask your mother, your spouse, or a close friend to help you. Adding a brief description of a few of your greatest gifts and talents to your LifeCreed, then listening to your own voice reminding you of them, will generate a powerful response in your mind-brain and in your life. If you don't feel comfortable asking anyone else, just imagine what positive things they would say about you if you did ask them. If you're a religious person, think about the positive things your Creator would have to say about you.

State each gift or talent briefly, simply, and in the first-person present tense. Place these in your LifeCreed wherever you feel appropriate. Some examples might be:

- I am a great listener.

- I have a unique ability to lift the spirit of everyone I meet.

- I am extremely creative and artistic.

- I have the gift of great faith.

- I have tremendous empathy for others.

- I'm really good with my hands and fixing things.

- I'm really smart with electronics.

3. **Slogans, quotes, lyrics, etc.:** Many of my clients have inserted slogans, quotes, song lyrics, etc., that they personally find inspirational or motivational. These can come from a variety of sources: scripture, famous people, novels, self-help titles, songs, movies, etc. One client is a big fan of the Lord of the Ring movies. In one scene, Gandalf, the wizard, is perched on a narrow rock bridge spanning a deep chasm. Facing off with a huge fiery beast, he slams his staff into the rock and boldly shouts, "You shall not

pass!" My client has inserted this into a section of his LifeCreed where he talks about achieving a significant goal in the face of staggering obstacles. Imagine the mental models this activates and the meaning it has in his mind-brain as he recalls that movie scene and imagines himself as Gandolf the fearless wizard!

Consider all the time and expense that goes into creating a powerful scene like this in a movie. And then think about how it makes you feel. Think about hearing an old song you heard first in High School, or on your first date with your sweetheart. Those emotions and feelings are available for you; you just need to connect them to the areas of your LifeCreed that need that extra emotional punch. While the mental model you create for a new goal may seem small to begin with, connecting it to a powerfully emotional mental model that already exists for you is the ultimate short-cut!

Add your favorites to your LifeCreed and keep adding as you find more—especially those that elicit deep feelings, emotions or meaning within you; those you would really like to start living in your own life. My parents used an axiom that became one of my favorites: *Any job worth doing is worth doing well.* Another favorite was quoted to me by Napoleon Hill: *Every adversity and every defeat carries with it the seed of an equivalent or greater benefit, if you look for it.*

4. **Privileged Place Moments:** Take time to remember those experiences in your life when you were deeply moved or greatly inspired, when your perspective was incredibly clear, when you perceived truth, when you felt the presence of God, when you

were incredibly motivated, positive and optimistic. These experiences can come to you while watching a movie, reading a book, listening to music, attending a speech or seminar. They can come during a special moment with spouse, children or friends, or while meditating, praying or attending church. These powerful moments can bring you to tears, raise your spirits to soaring heights, and fill you with resolve and a commitment to improve or take action. These are magical moments when you are fully in the *Privileged Place*.

Unfortunately, these moments are brief and intermittent. Before you know it the reality and immediacy of life crowds back in and the moment passes. But what if you could forever capture the magic and power of those moments? What if you could experience them over and over again? What if you could call on them to lift and strengthen you in times of trial and despair? You can.

Carry a small notebook or mini-digital recorder with you in your pocket at all times. This will become your *LifeCreed Ideas Notebook*. When you experience one of these inspiring, life-changing events, describe in detail what you saw, read or heard. Describe your insights, feelings and why it touched you so powerfully. Record how you believe you can use the information and what goals, commitments and resolutions it inspires you to make. Brief details can be recorded in your notebook, or recorder, and then expanded in your Feelings Journal. Then, take this information and integrate it into your LifeCreed.

Every time you listen to your LifeCreed you can relive these powerful experiences and be uplifted anew. Never allow the power of these sacred moments to be lost again. When they break

126

through the surface to the Privileged Place, capture them in your notebook or pocket recorder and then forever in your Feelings Journal and LifeCreed. It is easy to be satisfied to have these experiences just be fleeting moments. With the LifeBalance Tools they will be lasting and treasured experiences.

Now It's Your Turn

Exercise:

You now have everything you need to assemble the content for your first complete LifeCreed. Do the following:

1. Answer the LifeCreed Questions as instructed in this chapter and apply the Seven-Step Process to convert your answers to LifeCreed Statements.

2. Review the four categories of Additional LifeCreed Content and create LifeCreed Statements as you deem appropriate.

3. Review the Sample LifeCreeds section in the Appendix to obtain ideas for additional LifeCreed Statements and content for your LifeCreed.

4. Put all of the above in writing before proceeding to Chapter 13.

127

13

Record Your LifeCreed™

〜

You've arrived at the exciting point where you are ready to complete and record your LifeCreed.

Over your lifetime the voice you hear the most is your own. It is the voice that is most familiar to you. It is also the voice that you consider to be the most credible; you believe your own voice more than anyone else's. That is why what you say to yourself—both good and bad—is so critical! This may take some getting used to, but you will. One client had such a tough time getting accustomed to hearing her recorded voice that she decided to listen to her LifeCreed in the shower every morning. She would start the tape and then jump under the water in the shower to muffle the sound. She eventually became more comfortable with her own voice.

Studies show that your self-talk dramatically increases the meaning and credibility of any information as it enters your mind-brain. You will use the powerful mind-brain science of self-talk to your advantage by recording your LifeCreed in your own voice.

129

Many find the first recording of their LifeCreed a somewhat awkward experience. The following suggestions come from years of experience with thousands of clients. These 10 tips will help you through your first experience:

1. **Use your LifeCreed question responses:** Your recording will come directly from the LifeCreed question responses, additional ideas, or client samples you have converted into your own Life-Creed Statements. Simply use your handwritten notes or computer printout, of all the formatted pages you compiled through the Seven-Step Process and your work in Chapter 12. Remember, don't worry about the order. Simply put all of your LifeCreed Statements and content together in whatever way feels right to you.

2. **Choose the right setting:** It can be quite a challenge to find a quiet, private place to record your LifeCreed—phones ring, family members interrupt, you fear someone might overhear you. Ideally, you want to avoid all distractions. One secluded place to record your LifeCreed is in your car. It's quiet, private and usually has a built-in stereo system to play the accelerated-learning back-ground music. Avoid places where passing cars will be disruptive. Your garage or a secluded parking spot can work really well. If recording in your home or office, you may want to put up a "Do Not Disturb" sign on the door. The bathroom can even work for a recording session.

    Whatever you do, choose the location that would make it easiest for you to make the recording without interruption. Be sure to tell your spouse what you're going to do. (I had one client who went out to the garage, closed the garage door and got in his car. His wife thought for a moment he was trying to do himself in!)

3. **Gather equipment and materials:** Make certain you have everything assembled that you need to record your LifeCreed. Study out the operation of the equipment, check for fresh batteries and make sure your cassette tape is blank.

    Option #1: Recording in the car
    Tape recorder, battery operated
    CD Player in car
    Blank audiocassette tape
    CD with Accelerated-Learning Music
    LifeCreed Statements and content

    Option #2: Recording in the home or office
    Tape recorder
    CD Player
    Blank audiocassette tape
    CD with Accelerated-Learning Music
    LifeCreed Statements and content
    "Do Not Disturb" sign

4. **Make sure you're upbeat and positive:** When you record your LifeCreed, make certain you're in a state of mind where you're feeling positive, optimistic and enthusiastic. This attitude will be reflected in your voice and communicated to every cell in your mind-brain each time you listen to your LifeCreed. If you're having difficulty getting into this frame of mind, select a Life-Creed Statement and read it. Visualize how it will feel to be that person, accomplish that goal, or to be in that situation. Take

whatever time you need to feel the excitement again. Then you'll be ready.

In the future, if you are feeling negative, down or depressed, play your LifeCreed. Hearing your positive voice will give you a lift. Never underestimate the power of self-talk—positive or negative self-talk. When you find that your self-talk is down and negative, turn on your LifeCreed recording and let your positive self-talk dispel the negative.

5. **Rehearse beforehand:** Before you start recording, take a minute or two to rehearse. Read aloud from your LifeCreed Statement pages with the music playing in the background. Become familiar with what is there and comfortable with hearing yourself read it out loud.

6. **Choosing your music:** As we have already discussed, certain kinds of music can put the mind-brain into an accelerated-learning state. Larghetto or andante movements in Baroque concertos (a restful tempo of about 60 beats per minute) actually open up pathways and connections throughout the mind-brain, intensifying the formation and expansion of mental models. Baroque composers typically scored this peaceful, soothing music for string instruments. The LifeBalance Institute website contains a list of additional composers and specific arrangements that are appropriate. And, a CD containing samples of Accelerated-Learning Music is included with this book.

    Note: People invariably ask, "Can I substitute the classical CD's or tapes with some of my favorite tunes?" The answer is no. The choice of music has nothing to do with personal taste or entertainment value. Accelerated-Learning Music is used to evoke a specific psycho-physical state of relaxed concentration in the mind-brain, allowing for the unrestricted absorption of information.

7.   **Adjust the volume:** You'll need to experiment a little to find the proper balance between the volume of the music and your voice. After a minute or two of recording, you will notice on playback that, compared to the volume of your voice, the background music from your stereo is generally softer than you thought. To balance it out, turn the volume of the music up so it is just louder than that of your own voice. At first, speaking over the volume of the music will be a bit awkward. Experiment with different volumes until you get it right. When the proper recording balance is achieved, you should be able to hear your own voice just above the background music.

8.   **Get accustomed to the sound of your voice.** On first hearing the recording of their LifeCreed in their own voice, many people complain, "Does my voice really sound like that?" or "It sounds like I'm giving a funeral sermon." Don't worry about how the initial recording sounds. Remember, your LifeCreed is always evolving. You will modify and re-record your LifeCreed several times. As the months and years go by, you will come to appreciate and even enjoy hearing your own voice. You will become more comfortable and polished each time you make a new recording. Remember, your LifeCreed is for your ears only, so you needn't

be self-conscious or worry what others will think when you record it.

Important: You may have the inclination to keep re-recording until you get everything perfect—DON'T! Practice a few times, then make the recording, complete with stutters, mispronounced words, etc. Just get it done so you can start listening to it and begin the process. Your LifeCreed is not for motivational hype—it is intended to open your mind and continually feed it specific information and positive instructions.

9. **Leave a four-to five-second gap:** Your LifeCreed most often is divided into sections—a specific goal or ideal presented with its accompanying motive/meaning and hook—also known as a LifeCreed Statement. After each complete LifeCreed Statement, leave a four- to five-second gap of silence before you proceed to the next section. This gap allows your mind-brain to absorb the information before going on. As you listen daily to your Life-Creed, you will find during these periods of silence that you begin to visualize or see in your mind's eye the realization of your goal or ideal. During these gaps, ideas, insights and feelings likely will flood into your mind. Make sure you have a tape recorder or pen and pad handy to jot down these impressions as they come.

10. **Listen to your LifeCreed daily:** Listen to your LifeCreed twice daily for three weeks. You don't need to listen to your entire LifeCreed at one time. Just start the tape up where you left off. Soon you will begin to develop what is known as *Creed Nausea*—"If I have to listen to this one more time I think I'll be sick!"

134

At this point you will be ready to make the first LifeCreed revision as outlined in Chapter 14.

Important: Again, Your LifeCreed is For Your Eyes and Ears Only

Your LifeCreed is all about you and the realization of your ideal self and ideal life. If others were to read or listen to it they might not understand. With everything stated in first-person present tense as if you've already achieved it, they could interpret your LifeCreed as arrogant or silly. Suppose, for example, you are working at controlling your temper, so you create language in your LifeCreed to that effect. You state: "I'm in complete control of my voice and temper. My wife and children are in awe at how cool and calm I am under pressure. I feel great knowing I've overcome this hurtful habit in my life."

Now imagine your spouse gets hold of your LifeCreed and reads this or hears you saying it on your LifeCreed recording. Later that day you lose your temper with one of your children and your spouse eyes you with a look of, "I thought you were in total control of your temper and that you're in awe at how cool and calm you are!" It's like somebody just dropped chewed gum in your soup—it ruins the whole thing! Your LifeCreed is for your eyes and ears only.

How Do I Coordinate My LifeCreed With My Calendar?

You may be wondering how dates and times in your LifeCreed are coordinated with your daily calendar. Once you complete your LifeCreed, review it for any dates and times that should be entered in your daily schedule. Put these in your day-planning system (PDA, planner, computer, etc; you may want to use the reminder system on the LifeBalance Website).

Be sparing with the number of date and time hooks in your Life-Creed—you don't want to overload your daily schedule with a multitude of entries. If there are too many it becomes overwhelming and your mind-brain becomes desensitized to it.

For instance, one client scheduled out in minute detail many of the goals in his LifeCreed and entered them in his PDA with alarms attached. Multiple times each day his PDA alarm sounded off. After awhile he just started hitting the "cancel" button and pushing the scheduled activity back, putting it off until later. Too often he ended up forgetting about it all together.

So, rather than trying to schedule everything, only schedule on your calendar appointments and reminders for the most important goals in your LifeCreed; no more than a few each day. This way you can focus on a few at a time and not be overwhelmed. Over time, as these activities become a habit, or you accomplish the goal, you can replace them with a few more important items on your daily calendar.

Keep in mind that although many of your goals and ideals may not be physically entered on your daily calendar, just Feelings Journaling and listening to your LifeCreed on a daily basis will cause your mind-brain to naturally focus on many of your goals and bring them to fruition. Many of my clients are amazed when they get down the road and look back realizing they have achieved many of the goals in their LifeCreed without fully realizing it. Such is the power of the daily LifeCreed in the mind-brain habit formation and goal achievement processes.

～

Your LifeCreed is an amazing document. It defines the picture of yourself that you will carry in your heart each day, and is a constant reaffirmation of who you really are. It's the definition of yourself that everyone else will begin to see. As you begin the process of using your LifeCreed each day, hold on. You will be amazed at how your perspective of yourself and those around you begins to change. It's like getting new glasses. People will ask you "what's different about you?" Just smile and say "everything and nothing!"

Now It's Your Turn

Exercise:

Following the instructions in this chapter, record your first LifeCreed and begin listening to it twice daily for the next three weeks. **Note:** <u>Do not</u> procrastinate the recording of your LifeCreed because you want it to be perfect. Just get the first recording done as quickly as possible so you can begin listening to it and receiving the amazing benefits. After three weeks you will be able to make all of the corrections you desire and then re-record your LifeCreed.

Because I have had such great results, I know it's just a matter of deciding, detailing it in my Creed, knowing the cost involved, and then knowing it will happen soon! —J. Scarpo

14

Your Ever-Evolving LifeCreed™

Is it true that you *can't teach old dogs new tricks*? Many "old dogs" have tried the LifeBalance System—many who really doubted their ability to make a significant and lasting change in their lives. Many had tried a multitude of self-improvement programs, with minimal success and much frustration, but with the LifeBalance System they achieved remarkable results.

The reason most people don't succeed in making the changes they desire is they lack the understanding of a simple, practical, daily system and the necessary tools to make needed changes in their lives. The LifeCreed is a simple and powerful tool you can use everyday for the rest of your life to continue changing and evolving in every facet of your life. Each time you want to change a specific habit, achieve a certain goal, progress to a new level, integrate this desire into your Feelings Journal and LifeCreed and it will become a reality.

Can a person really, truly, permanently change? Yes—in wonderful and amazing ways! With your LifeCreed, your upward spiraling evolution will never end. You can begin this evolutionary process with the first revision of your LifeCreed.

Revising Your LifeCreed

After approximately three weeks of listening to your initial LifeCreed recording, *Creed nausea* will start to set in with certain parts of your LifeCreed and you will be ready to revise it. Follow these guidelines:

1. **Read and Listen:** Sit down with a written copy of your LifeCreed and follow along as you listen to your LifeCreed recording. It's very important that you listen and read at the same time. Do not review your written LifeCreed without simultaneously listening to the recording. This will give you the best feedback regarding which parts you want to change.

2. **Edit As You Go:** Draw lines through the parts that have become irritating or boring; that you want to eliminate. Circle those you want to revise or expand. Make notes in the margins, indicating what revisions or additions you have in mind.

3. **Listen for Voice Revisions:** Make note of places where your voice sounds monotone or tedious, where you could add more inflection, enthusiasm, speed up or pause.

4. **Review Your LifeCreed Ideas Notebook:** This is the notebook you've been keeping with ideas for your LifeCreed revisions. Daily, as you listen to your LifeCreed and keep your Feelings Journal, ideas for additions to your LifeCreed will come to you. In addition, you will have special *Privileged Place Moments*. Use

your LifeCreed Ideas Notebook for recording these ideas. Add these ideas to the appropriate places on the written copy of your LifeCreed. Remember; don't worry about dividing your new ideas and revisions into sections like family, financial, physical, etc. Place new additions in various locations throughout your Life-Creed, depending on what makes the most sense and feels good to you, and what will create the most powerful meaning and motive. For example, statements about God, your spouse, your children, may be placed in various sections of your Creed because they are an integral part of many areas of your life.

5. **Jot down Self-improvement Ideas:** Over the years you've probably read a number of self-improvement books or attended seminars and gleaned some great ideas. At the time you probably thought, "I'd really like to implement that in my life" or "If I could just do that, my life would be so much better." The same thing may happen to you when you listen to religious ministers or leaders, listen to good programs on the radio or watch uplifting TV programs. The moment you come across these ideas, write them down in your LifeCreed Ideas Notebook so you can include them in the next revision of your LifeCreed. Once in your LifeCreed, you will start living them—guaranteed!

6. **Borrow Ideas From Others:** Review the sample LifeCreeds of my clients in the Appendix to get additional ideas and insights for refining your LifeCreed. Feel free to borrow from other sources as much as you like. Eventually, you will take others' ideas, extrapolate them, revise them, and finally put them into your own words and make them a part of your LifeCreed.

7. **Restructuring LifeCreed Statements That Lack Power:** After you have listened to your LifeCreed for three weeks, you may find that some of your LifeCreed Statements (Self-Directed Goals) lack power. This could be manifest in several ways:

- The Statement has become boring and does not elicit much if any emotional response in your mind-brain.

- You don't know if you really want to achieve the stated goal or not.

- You're having trouble visualizing or believing that you will ever achieve the stated goal.

If you experience any of the above, proceed as follows:

a. Feelings Journal about the LifeCreed Statement in question. If it has become boring, why? What can you revise or add to give it more meaning and emotional connections? Do you really want to achieve the goal? If you do, why? Expand on your motive. Visualize yourself already having achieved it and state in detail how you feel; what your life is like. Attach as much powerful meaning to the goal as possible.

b. If you are having trouble believing that you will ever achieve the stated goal, Feelings Journal about why you are having this challenge. What are the obstacles standing in your way? What can you do to overcome those obstacles? Perhaps your goal is too big a step at one time. How can you break it down into smaller steps or sequential goals—"One year from now on June 1ˢᵗ, I have _____." Two years from now on June 1ˢᵗ, I have _____."

Maybe your doubts are based on flawed beliefs, habitual ways of thinking, a lack of self confidence, or other dominant negative mental models. Perhaps you can state the goal as a "process" that takes place gradually over time as opposed to all at once— "Each day I become more _____." "Daily I create the environment where I can _____." Be sure you attach a complete motive and hooks to these statements.

c. From your Feelings Journaling, revise your LifeCreed Statement. If you discover that you really don't want to pursue the goal, eliminate it. If the goal needs more meaning, add it. If there are obstacles, state them and how (*hooks*) you will overcome them. If the goal is too big a step all at once, break it down into smaller goals and create a complete LifeCreed Statement for each one.

8. **Draft Your Updated Version:** Using the edited copy of your original LifeCreed (with all the scribbled notes, corrections and additions you have made) write or type your new, updated LifeCreed. Make certain you carefully follow the Seven-Step Process for LifeCreed Statement formation outlined in Chapter 11.

9. **Record Your Revised LifeCreed:** Record your revised LifeCreed following the same steps used to record your initial LifeCreed. However, this time, as per your notes, see if you can add enthusi-

asm to parts that seemed boring in your first recording, read it with more emphasis, add inflection, etc.

10. **Maintain a Positive Frame of Mind:** As before, record your revised LifeCreed when you are feeling positive, optimistic and enthusiastic. This attitude will be reflected in your voice and communicated to your mind-brain every time you listen to it.

Future revisions of your LifeCreed

Every three to four months or as needed during the first year, repeat the entire process outlined in this chapter to further refine your LifeCreed. In the second year, repeat the LifeCreed revision process only every six to eight months, or as needed. From the third year on, you'll probably revise your LifeCreed about once a year. However, any time you feel the need to change or add to your LifeCreed, don't hesitate to do so. As you accomplish goals and see ideals realized, add new ones.

As you continue to use all of the tools and resources in the Life-Balance System, you will discover even more additions for your future LifeCreed revisions. Your LifeCreed will become part of an upward spiraling pattern of success and happiness that will last a lifetime.

Note: Always remember that your LifeCreed is a vehicle to which you can attach any goal, ideal, principle, practice or desire you want to achieve and make a permanent part of your life. Anytime in the future, when a new idea or desire hits you, or when you discover a new principle, seek a new direction or for any reason find yourself thinking about a change or improvement you'd like to make, simply Feelings Journal about it, add it to your LifeCreed, then watch it become a reality!

Be sure to save the written versions of your old LifeCreeds. It is so enlightening and motivating to see how your thoughts and habits evolve over the years.

Now it's your turn

Within the next three to four weeks, when Creed nausea begins to set in, schedule several hours to revise your LifeCreed. Be sure to calendar this time as a "must-do" appointment or you will likely procrastinate. This becomes a problem when people grow nauseated with their initial LifeCreed and stop listening to it with the full intention of doing the revision. Before they know it, months have passed and they don't have a revised LifeCreed, nor have they been listening to their old LifeCreed. This is how people fall out of the LifeBalance System and back into old habits and ruts.

With the Byte I know I can create instant and powerful mental force to take immediate control of my conscious thoughts. This is the best tool I have ever used in the battle against my compulsive nature and addictive tendencies.

—Chris J.

As she listened to her LifeCreed and reviewed the Byte, a miracle began to unfold: her attitude and feelings toward Jack began to change. Today she and Jack have one of the most beautiful love affairs you can imagine.

—Leo Weidner

146

15

Tool #3: The Byte—Instant On-the-Spot Success!

Many people have negative feelings or behaviors so deeply dominant and entrenched that these cause major disruptions in their lives and relationships. No matter how hard they try, in the heat of the moment, in certain situations, in the presence of certain stimuli, the negative feelings and behaviors are automatically triggered. Many clients have declared, "If I could just find a way to overcome this, my life would be so much better."

The Power of The Byte

You have learned how to use Feelings Journaling and the LifeCreed to overcome virtually any dominant mental model and habit in your life. You have begun a wonderful process that will lead to great rewards. You may have identified specific aspects of your life that need special attention. There may be relationships that need a jumpstart, or particular habits that are wearing you down. If you have an urgency to find relief in your life right now, you can do so with *The Byte.*

In computer language, a *byte* is a small unit of information that gives the computer a command to do something specific. In the Life-Balance system, *The Byte* is designed to give your brain a specific command and instantly generate an enormous amount of mental force, activating the mental model you desire, on the spot.

How do you know when to use one?

When you have a habit or feeling that is interfering with your personal growth, happiness or an important relationship, you need to use The Byte. The source for the content of your Byte may come from your LifeCreed, or it may come from a life experience and be something you end up adding to your LifeCreed. Either way, The Byte is designed to meet a specific need until the negative habit or feeling is conquered.

The power of The Byte resides in the fact that your mind cannot focus on two dissimilar thoughts at one time; it can't access two opposing mental models at once. When your mind is dominated by negative thoughts, you can introduce The Byte to dispel and replace these thoughts with positive thoughts of your choosing.

Getting Started on Your First Byte

The most common use for The Byte is in personal relationships. A client recently wrote me:

"Just a few weeks ago you shared this powerful tool with me. The Byte really helped me in dealing with a difficult situation with a coworker. Then, just a few days ago, I was speaking with my uncle.

He's had some real problems in dealing with his kids,, and once again things had flared up. Being a "neutral" party, I am often in the middle of trying to find some common ground, and help him to figure out how to make things right. But what I recognized, after working with the LifeBalance System, was his desire to change everyone else, so he could get along with them. We talked about this for awhile, and I was able, by utilizing The Byte, to show him the power of changing his perception of them, rather than trying so hard to change them. I told him to make a list of all the positive attributes of each of his kids, and any time he was dealing with them, to reflect on this list first, and then decide how to proceed. It really made a difference. He couldn't stop with all the positive things he had to say about them. His concerns and issues seemed so small in comparison. This little tool has been a life saver."

This client was using the most basic form of The Byte. He was having difficulties in his relationships because his negative feelings were getting in the way. We've all been confronted with this. There are some people that no matter how hard we try, we just can't seem to have a complete, positive conversation with them. Or, no matter how a conversation starts, it always seems to end in the same old tired argument. It may even be that the other party is difficult to deal with, or even wrong. The power of The Byte is in taking charge of our half of the relationship in order to positively affect the whole of it.

The Byte may seem simple, but it has far-reaching abilities and power. It may surprise you just how easy it is to create and implement. You start with a blank piece of paper and an open mind. Begin by putting the name of the person with whom you want to improve your relationship at the top of the page. Then make a list of all their positive attributes or things you appreciate about them. Write down a positive experience you've shared or an event that caused you to admire or feel close to this person. If you don't have one, imagine what that would be like, and in as much detail as possible, write it down. There it is—*The Byte.*

Write the list of positive attributes and the positive experience on a 3 x 5 card you carry with you. Then, when you're in a situation where you're interacting with this person, reflect on your Byte and hold it in your conscious thoughts. Don't let the person see the card, or tell them what's on it. It's more powerful for them to just feel the positive energy as you hold those thoughts in your mind.

Many clients who use this tool report back how much the other person begins to change. In actuality, the perception of the client changed first, and then the other person adjusted to fit that new and positive perception. It's amazing how quickly this simple little tool begins to positively improve relationships.

Creating and Using a Byte
Whenever You Need One

A properly constructed Byte is remarkably powerful. It is your *super-charged tool for instant change*. Follow these simple steps whenever you need a Byte:

- **Write the Polar Opposite of Your Negative Thought or Habit:** In choosing the content for your Byte, you must select something that is the positive polar opposite of the negative thought or behavior you are trying to dispel. For example, if you have trouble with negative or pessimistic thoughts about your new business, your Byte should contain descriptions of the most positive things about your new business, or your vision of them in the future. If you become angry around your teenage son because you automatically think of all his flaws, your Byte should contain descriptions of his most outstanding qualities. If you have a habit of feeling fear or doubt in certain situations, your Byte should contain descriptions of you as a powerful and courageous person. Be sure to state everything in the present tense.

- **Connect to Deep Emotions, Feelings and Meaning:** Like advertisers and Hollywood, you want the descriptions in your Byte to activate existing mental models that are filled with powerful memories, emotions, feeling and meaning. When you review or think about your Byte it should immediately take over the stage of your conscious mind.

  You need to give your conscious attention a place of deep meaning to go to, directing it away from the old dominant habit. This place of deep meaning is created when your Byte triggers powerful emotions. If reading your Byte sends chills up your spine, makes your hair stand up on end, brings you to tears, or fills you with an uplifting spirit or inspiration, then your Byte is constructed properly. Again, make sure everything is stated in the present tense.

How to Use The Byte

- **Make it Portable and Accessible:** You don't always know when your negative thoughts, behaviors or habits will hit you. You need to be prepared to use your Byte at any time. Record your Byte on a 3 x 5 card and carry it with you at all times. When you feel negative thoughts beginning to invade your mind you can instantly access and employ your Byte to dispel them. In essence you are turning lemons into lemonade. After awhile, the undesired thoughts and behavior will stop and you will automatically choose the new thoughts and behavior you desire.

- **Enter the *Privileged Place*:** The instant you sense your undesired thoughts entering your mind, immediately take out your Byte and read and focus on it intensely. Visualize what you are reading. Keep The Byte on the stage of your mind, hold it there in the Privileged Place until the undesired thoughts dissipate and are gone. Don't give in to the undesired thoughts or behaviors or give up too soon. If you stay focused on your Byte while in the Privileged Place, the mental force generated by your positive thoughts will win out.

- **Get accustomed to Using The Byte:** Develop a habit of turning to The Byte to fortify, inspire and focus. You'll find you have increased capacity to derail negative thoughts, feelings, and habits.

- **Add The Byte to Your LifeCreed:** Place the content of The Byte in your LifeCreed. Also put an instruction in your LifeCreed that whenever the undesired thoughts you are trying to overcome enter your mind, you take out The Byte and review it. Describe how you feel as you review The Byte and how this is overcoming your negative habit.

16

Direct Life-Applications for The Byte

~

You can apply the power of The Byte to virtually any area of your life you want to immediately change or improve. It is especially effective in modifying your feelings and behaviors in troubled relationships.

The Byte Saved Their Marriage

Several years ago one client's husband had committed a serious betrayal in their marriage causing her severe mental and emotional anguish. She harbored enormous hurt and resentment, but her husband was humble and apologetic. She was willing to see if the relationship could be saved. She worked on focusing on "Jack #2," the repentant and striving man she is married to now, rather than "Jack #1," the man who had betrayed her. It was difficult at first, but eventually she was able to look back on all of her husband's good qualities—the things she admired most in him when they first fell in love." She Feelings Journaled about these thoughts and made a list of Jack's finest qualities.

As she worked on this she remembered a time when they were on vacation in South America and Jack was interacting with some of the local people. She recalls, "As I watched I was amazed at his compassion, inspiring words, and the way he uplifted and loved those people. I was so proud of him and my heart was filled with so much love for him."

She took that experience and wrote about it in as much detail as she could, with full emotion, and in the present tense as if she were there observing it all over again. Whenever she found her mind dominated by thoughts of Jack's betrayal, she would take out the list of his qualities, and the written description of her experience with him in South America and read it. Each time it would bring back all those wonderful feelings. She would visualize herself observing Jack and allow all the emotions of love and appreciation to wash over her. She also added the South America experience to her LifeCreed. As she listened to her LifeCreed and reviewed The Byte, a miracle began to unfold: Her attitude and feelings toward Jack began to change and soften. Today she and Jack have one of the most beautiful love affairs you can imagine.

Transference of Thought

In numerous studies over the last several decades, scientists have clearly shown that *thoughts are things*. In other words, the thoughts you allow to act on the stage of your mind create energy and messages that are transferred to the people around you. This process operates the same for negative and positive thoughts.

As a relationship deteriorates, the minds of the individuals involved become increasingly dominated by negative thoughts. After awhile, others can "feel" the negative energy and sense the negative thoughts without any words being spoken. In fact, these negative thoughts can be transferred over great distances.

The same holds true for positive thoughts about other people. The energy and message of positive thoughts are transferred without any words expressed. Consider just one of numerous examples:

When Ghandi was asked how he was able to lead India to independence from the British Empire he indicated it was not what they said, although that was important, nor what they did, but is was their "being ness" their "collective intent" that brought about such a miraculous result.

Many clients have tested and proven this. One man was having serious marital problems after twenty years of marriage. He created a Byte consisting of:

a. A list of his wife's great qualities, the things he loves and admires most, the reasons he married her in the first place, and

b. A detailed description of his most cherished experience with his wife, a time when he felt the greatest amount of love, admiration, appreciation and closeness.

He said nothing about The Byte to his wife. Whenever unflattering thoughts about his wife came into his mind, he would take out his Byte, review it and dwell on it. As his thoughts became more positive, his attitude toward his wife began to change. Over time, his wife began to be influenced by his powerfully positive attitude and her demeanor and attitudes also began to change. Their marriage improved significantly.

Whether you're at home, at work, or across the globe, the Byte will generate powerful thoughts that are communicated to those you care about most.

Instant Mental Model Change

Sometimes change is slow and incremental. Other times, it's like a light suddenly turning on in a dark room. That's what happened to one Marine who was allowing a small irritation to disrupt an otherwise wonderful marriage. During a LifeBalance training session with the US Marine Corps, participants were asked to think of a negative attitude or behavior in their life that they would like to change. Here's what happened:

> A hand went up. It was Anthony, a big, lean and rugged man, just what you would likely picture when you think of *The Few, the Proud, the Marines*. "Yeah, I'll tell you something. The trash!" he blurted out. Puzzled, the whole group waited for an explanation. "The trash! My wife is always naggin' on me to get the trash out the night before pick-up. What's the big deal? I always get it out in the morning in time for the trash collectors. What does it matter when I do it so long as I do it? Why does she have to have it out the night before? It drives me crazy! We've been fighting about this our whole marriage."

> The LifeBalance trainers and the other Marines spent 20 minutes trying to reason with Anthony about how it was such a small thing, that he should just let his wife have her way. But he wouldn't budge. He just couldn't get out of his dominant mental model regarding the trash—he kept automatically selecting that mental model over and over again. During the

156

break I sat with Anthony and instructed him to create a Byte for the situation. I asked him to journal his feelings about all the wonderful qualities he admired in his wife; why he loved her; what motivated him to marry her in the first place. I asked him to remember an experience when his love, admiration and respect for her were deeper than ever. He spent the break writing all these feelings out.

After the break we listened to a special music set and it was time to close for the day. Suddenly Anthony asked if he could say something to the group. This big, tough Marine stood up and with a slight quiver in his voice he said, "I can't believe what a jerk I've been! How could I have been so stubborn about a stupid little thing like the trash? What was I thinking? My wife is a queen. I should be washing her feet when she comes home from work."

The room was silent. We all just sat with our mouths open and stared. Suddenly the entire group broke out in applause for Anthony! We all had witnessed the power of Feelings Journaling and The Byte to generate mental force and switch Anthony to a completely different mental model! If he ever has negative thoughts about his wife and the trash issue, all he needs to do is pull out his Byte and switch mental models.

Many Relationship Applications for *The Byte*

The Byte is a wonderful tool to restore love and harmony to a marital relationship. The Byte can also be used to restore any important relationship. For example:

- Negative feelings toward a teenage child who has rebelled and caused the family pain and disruption.

- Resentment toward a parent who caused you pain as a child.

- Bitter feelings for a brother or sister, or for extended family members.

- Bad feelings for a boss, colleague or fellow-employee.

- Negative feelings toward yourself for past mistakes or failures.

In Business

I have a client in the insurance business that hated to talk with people on the phone, but he loved working with people face-to-face. Whenever he had to make sales or client follow-up calls on the telephone his mind would fill with negative thoughts and fears. First I instructed him to Feelings Journal and get out all his negative feelings about making calls. Then I had him Feelings Journal about all of the gifts and talents that made him so effective when he was face-to-face with people. I also had him describe all the reasons why he loved meeting with people, the unique services he provided to them, and why they appreciated him so much. From these journal entries he extrapolated his Byte and additions for his LifeCreed.

Before each phone calling session, he reviewed, visualized and experienced the feelings of his Byte. He made all his calls one day each week. After six weeks he called me and said "Leo, I woke up this morning and I'm really excited about talking with people on the phone! I can't believe I'm saying this but it's how I feel."

Key: When he told me how excited he was I immediately responded, "Write down exactly what you're feeling. Capture the excitement of this experience right now." "Why?" he asked. "Because down the road you're going to have an off day when some of your negative feelings about the phone return. By capturing the full emotion of your excitement and adding it to your Byte and LifeCreed, you'll be able to rid yourself of the negative thoughts when they come."

Over time his mental model and the meaning of the telephone changed from "I hate to talk to people on the phone" to "I have a powerful motive for talking with people on the phone and I love it!"

A Presentation, Speech or Performance

Competitive athletes are trained to use a similar process to what we call The Byte. As they prepare for an event, they visualize their performance in their mind over and over again. They see and feel themselves crossing the finish line first, giving a perfect 10 performance, or scoring the winning goal. They literally experience the emotions of standing on the podium and receiving the gold medal, holding up the trophy to the cheer of the crowd. Whenever doubts, fears or discouragement enter their mind, they dispel and replace them by playing their Byte.

The great golfer, Johnny Miller described how before every swing he would visualize the perfect outcome he desired: the ball leaving his club; the trajectory it would follow; the exact spot where it would land. His enormous success using what I call the Byte speaks for itself.

You can do the same thing when preparing for an important presentation, speech, interview, etc. See yourself doing it perfectly. Write down the feelings you have as everyone claps, congratulates you, awards you the sale, gives you the job. As you prepare, read and visualize this Byte over and over again. Any time doubts or fears arise, dispel and replace them with your Byte.

Compulsive Behaviors and Addictions

Growing numbers of people suffer from compulsive behaviors and addictions. They describe a wave or overwhelming urge that suddenly washes over them to indulge in their addictive behavior. Once this urge hits, tying to control it can be extremely difficult, or virtually impossible. If this describes your situation, create a Byte. Do it when you are under control and free of the urge to act out your addiction. Your Byte could be a list of all the positive benefits you would have in your life if you were free of your addiction. It could be a letter to yourself giving you words of encouragement and a powerful symbol or message to change your mental model and thought pattern. Consider some real-life examples from among my clients and the Bytes they created:

"I Promise You"

I have a client who had a drinking problem. He tried time and time again to stop without success. I suggested he create a Byte. What would stimulate meaning and motive so powerful to his mind-brain that it would override his craving for alcohol and shift him to a new mental model?

First I suggested he promise his wife that he would quit. He indicated he had done that many times and it had failed. I asked him, "Do you really want to stop?" "Yes" he insisted. In our conversation I discovered he had an extremely close relationship with his son who

160

was the apple of his eye. I suggested he promise his son that he had seen his dad drink for the last time. I suggested he take a photograph of his son and on the bottom of it write the words "I promise you." He was to put this photo in his wallet so that if he went to the liquor store to buy a bottle he would have to see the photo when getting out his money.

He was stunned by this suggestion. He was so angry at me for making the suggestion he didn't speak to me for 10 days (now that's powerful meaning!) But, he came back and agreed to use the photo and promise to his son as his Byte. In addition to the Byte, he had a statement regarding his alcoholism in his LifeCreed and he Feelings Journaled about it regularly. From that point forward he remained alcohol-free. I recently received a card from him. In part it read:

I have 6½ years of sobriety. Thanks! I am now 4 years a consecutive Top of the Table qualifier, 6 years Chairman of the Table and 14 years MDRT member. Thanks! (These are very prestigious awards/ positions in the insurance business.) I am in good shape—I run a 5K every single night. Thanks! Annie still loves me and is the center of my world. Thanks! Robbie is my close and wonderful son. Thanks! I am alive. Thanks! P.S. You still aggravate me. Thanks!

"I Am a Non-Smoker"

During a LifeBalance Institute weekend retreat, we were training the audience in the use of the Byte. One participant, Patty, had been a smoker for over twenty-two years. She had tried to quit many times without any lasting success. Patty created a Byte to counter her craving for cigarettes.

Understanding the power of motive and meaning in the mind-brain, Patty's Byte contained the following:

1. It began with the statement "I am a non-smoker."

2. It contained an instruction for her to clearly and vividly visualize her lungs as completely clean and vibrant as she repeated the word "breathe."

3. It included a detailed description of her vision of a long and healthy life, enjoying her children and her future grand-children.

4. It also contained her commitment to her children to be a non-smoker and a vivid description of the admiration on their bright, smiling faces as they congratulated her for being free of her addiction.

From that weekend forward, Patty has not smoked another cigarette. Never doubt the power of motive and meaning in the mind-brain!

A Priest and Pornography

With the advent of the Internet, an epidemic of pornography addiction is sweeping across America, and much of the world. One of our LifeBalance clients is a religious minister. Like millions of other professionals in America, and a growing number of ministers and priests, he got hooked on Internet pornography as a way to self-medicate and escape from the stress and pressures of life. Fortunately he entered a recovery program and was able to get his life and marriage back on track. But he still suffered from the side-effects of pornography exposure—the dominant mental model that had been formed. This mental model was interfering with his ability to have normal, healthy social and professional relationships with women. Seeing a woman in public, any woman, would often trigger pornographic images in his mind, causing him to view and think about women inappropriately; to view them as objects or a collection of physical body parts, rather than as holistic human beings. As you can imagine, this was tremendously frustrating and disruptive in his personal and professional life.

Through the LifeBalance training he learned how to create a Byte. The following is a copy of his Byte:

> "I view all women as my spiritual sisters, children of God. As their brother, they can trust me to protect them from all types of exploitation, abuse and harm. Whenever I have inappropriate thoughts pounding on the door of my mind's stage, I ask myself, "If that woman were suddenly injured or collapsed with a heart attack right here and now, could I call upon the power of God to save her, with pornographic thoughts in my mind?" I visualize myself looking into her eyes and praying to God to help her, his daughter and my sister."

Imagine the power of the mental model activated in the mind-brain of this minister by reading and visualizing his Byte! Over time, after repeatedly utilizing his Byte, he was able to look upon women in this healthy way automatically—his new mental model became dominant and he no longer had to think about it.

The grand key to the Byte is that it can instantly create meaning and motive stronger than that of the negative thought or desire you're trying to dispel and replace. Use the Byte to immediately begin overcoming a particular negative thought pattern, behavior or habit that is disrupting your life.

Note: The Byte does not replace professional therapy, recovery programs, support groups and other interventions that are so crucial to those suffering from addictions and other serious disorders. The Byte is intended as a support and additional tool that can be used in conjunction with these essential resources.

Mother Teresa said: "We can all do a small thing with great love." The Byte, by definition is a small thing; a small thing that will create a big difference in your life. Through the years some of the most emotional experiences I have shared with clients have involved the Byte. This "pocket-sized" tool for improving relationships and changing habits will bring positive change for you as it has for so many of my friends.

Now It's Your Turn

1. Select a specific thought process or behavior pattern that is disrupting your life.

2. Follow the guidelines in this chapter to formulate a *Byte* to counter this negative habit.

3. Carry this Byte with you and access it immediately whenever you sense the first signs of your negative thought or habit coming on.

4. Add The Byte to your LifeCreed as instructed in the chapter.

17

Revealing Wonder in Your Life

~

A client recently shared the following experience with me:

"I still remember the Christmas morning when I was seven years old. I had been watching one package under the tree for weeks. I knew what it was, but hidden behind the red and green wrapping paper, it seemed elusive and powerful. When the time finally came to open our presents, my Grandfather, who loved to do the honors, called each of us by name and handed over our prize. Being the oldest, I was first. As he handed me my wrapped treasure, the breath caught in my throat. I could hardly compose myself to find the edge of the wrapping paper and begin. But, in a flash the paper was gone, and a wooden box remained. This box held the mysteries of the universe. With these ingredients, I could create anything. It was a chemistry set.

Used properly, it contained everything necessary to create pungent smoke, turn red liquid to blue, and produce invisible ink. For weeks I worked with my chemistry set. I followed all the instructions, and did every "magic" trick.

When I was twelve I discovered my chemistry set again, in a pile of discarded trash. The magic was gone. The few weeks of discovery replaced by a sense of lost dreams. All the hope that had been contained in this wooden treasure chest had evaporated. Where had it gone?

Over the years this event seemed a metaphor for my life. Lots of promise and excitement, but soon replaced by the awful truth that it was all just sulphur powder and iodine, no magic and no miracles. I wandered like this for too much of my life, optimistic enough to believe, but defeated enough to give up. I had finally come to the place where no idea seemed powerful enough, and hope was just an excuse.

Then I discovered the LifeBalance System. Like many people who come to you Leo, I began because I had no better plan. If this had helped thousands of others, maybe, just maybe it could help me. And the only real alternative seemed to be giving up, so what did I have to lose? So I gave it a try, and You and the LifeBalance System changed my life in ways that still amaze me to this day.

In trying to summarize in my own mind the power of the LifeBalance System, I thought back to a chemistry class I took in college. Using essentially the same elements and basic tools contained in that wooden box I received as a child for Christmas, I learned amazing truths about what created our world, and continues to transform it. Using the same simple, basic building blocks, remarkable wonders were revealed. What I discovered was that my old chemistry set really did have all the answers. The components were there all along. What I have discovered through the LifeBalance System is that I already have all of the natural built-in abilities I need to succeed in every part of my life. All I needed was a daily system and tools to bring it all to life."

The *LifeBalance System* contains all the components to reveal wonder in your life. It has been proven with thousands of individuals, but the most important success story will be yours. Embrace the concepts presented here, and allow yourself to dream, to achieve.

I anxiously await your success stories.

Appendix

Mind-brain Science

~

This appendix and the many descriptions and applications of mind-brain science throughout this book are the result of thousands of hours of research and application over many years by Mark Kastleman. Mark's writing is inspired by the noble and courageous work of some of the world's leading neuroscientists and neurophysiologists. The purpose of this Appendix is to provide you with an in-depth summary of the cutting-edge mind-brain science behind the extraordinary effectiveness of the LifeBalance System and Tools.

With tremendous admiration and gratitude, Mark and Leo also wish to give special recognition to their dear friend, Dr. Page Bailey. A world-renowned psychologist and therapist, Page has dedicated his life to helping people understand and implement original methods and processes through which they can consciously direct their mind-brain to overcome addiction, chronic illness, chronic pain, negative habits, and achieve success in every aspect of life. The results Page has helped people around the world achieve are nothing short of miraculous. His influence, tutelage and mentoring have had a profound effect on Mark

Kastleman and Leo Weidner. Without Dr. Bailey, the critical integration of mind-brain science into this book would not have been possible.

What is *Mind-brain?*

When first hearing the term *mind-brain,* many people ask, "aren't the mind and the brain the same thing?" The answer is "No!" Neuroscience and neuropsychology have proven irrefutably that the *mind* is not the *brain,* and the *brain* is not the *mind*—each is separate and distinct, yet fully integrated. The brain is the physical two-hemisphere marvel in the body that we all are familiar with. The mind is our consciousness or what some have even called our spirit. Our mind forms a communication system that is present in every part of our brain and body. The 1980s and 1990s were called the "decades of the brain" by many. We are now in the "decade of the mind." Neuroscience has proven that through the power of our mind, we can literally change the physical structure of our brain! Through what is now called *directed mental force* or the power of directed thought, brain history can be altered—"mind over matter" is a reality! In this appendix you will learn the latest science behind harnessing and directing the power of your mind.

Why Is It So Difficult To Change?

Have you ever been introduced to a great self-improvement idea from a book, tape, radio or TV program, or seminar and excitedly thought to yourself, "If I could just find a way to integrate that into my life what a positive difference it would make?" You write the idea down and set a goal to start living it. Perhaps it's a strategy to lose weight, improve your marriage, reduce your stress, make more money, or communicate better with your children. The point is, when you first hear the idea you're excited, you really want to do it! But after a few days or weeks your enthusiasm wanes and you end up right back in the same old rut and routine. Why? Why is it so difficult to make a change? The answer is the *power of habits*.

The reason people have such a difficult time changing is due to the enormous power of habits. From the moment of your birth, your mind-brain seeks to turn every important activity and tendency into a habit. Your mind-brain seeks to automate everything you do. Once something is mastered and becomes "automatic" the mind-brain can direct its resources and energies to learning new skills. This is called the *principle of efficiency* and it is the mind-brain's number one goal. Think of all the things you learned as a child that you now do automatically: tying your shoes, writing your name, riding a bike. Imagine what would happen if every time you wanted to perform a common task your mind-brain had to master it all over again?

In his book, *A Universe of Consciousness*, Dr. Gerald Edelman quotes Henry Maudsley: "If an act became no easier after being done several times, if the careful direction of consciousness were necessary to its accomplishments in each occasion, it is evident that the whole activity of a lifetime might be confined to one or two deeds."

Were it not for the power and efficiency of habits, we would accomplish very little in life.

Change is difficult because the mind-brain expends enormous time and energy to develop habits. Asking the mind-brain to go back and change a habit—something it has worked so hard to make automatic—is asking a lot; it goes against the mind-brain's natural and dominant goal of efficiency. The mind-brain jealously guards its habits and doesn't change them quickly or easily.

You already have natural built-in habit-forming mechanisms and skills you have been using since the day you were born. You are amazingly effective and efficient at forming habits. Unfortunately, most of your habits have been formed unconsciously, without you being aware of the process. What if you could learn how to consciously and purposely direct your natural habit-forming processes to eliminate your negative behaviors and attain the life, success and relationships you desire?

In order to harness and direct your powerful habit-formation abilities, you must first learn how these processes operate in your mind-brain.

The Power of Mental Models

Through your genetic make-up you have inherited the tendency to form what are known as *totalities*. From the day of your birth, and perhaps even in the womb, your mind-brain has been taking everything you experience and using it to build a vast network of connections that Nobel Prize recipient, Dr. Gerald M. Edelman calls a *Dynamic Core*. Within this Dynamic Core, your mind-brain builds specific groups of connections known as *mental models*. It is through these mental models that everything you experience is interpreted and given meaning.

To illustrate the operation of mental models, Page Bailey has created the following exercise:

If I ask you to connect these three dots, how would you do it?

●

●   ●

If you're like most people, you immediately visualized a triangle. How did you get a triangle from three dots? You've just experienced the result of a mental model. As the three dots were processed through the appropriate mental model, you instantly perceived a triangle. For you, the meaning of the three dots is a triangle.

This mental model process can be illustrated as follows:

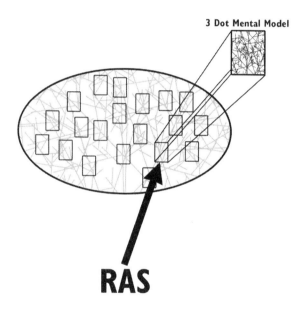

3 Dot Mental Model

RAS

Connections = Mental Models

Within your mind-brain are virtually limitless connections linked to everything you've ever experienced, and these connections are constantly expanding. Specific groups of these connections form mental models.

The RAS: Your Air Traffic Controller

At the base of your brain is the Reticular Activating System or RAS. Your RAS is like an air-traffic controller. In any given situation it decides which of all the vast number of your mental models to activate. Unless you force it to do otherwise, your RAS will always choose the mental model that is the most dominant for the given situation. When you see the three dots, the image is routed through your eyes to your RAS and then to the most dominant mental model; the one you have accessed most in the past to interpret what the three dots mean.

When you first saw the three dots, why didn't you immediately visualize the following:

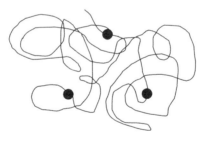

The reason you didn't choose this option for connecting the dots is that you have never seen it before; you don't have a mental model for interpreting the three dots in this manner. However, now that you have seen this new way of connecting the three dots, you will never be fooled by this exercise again. Your "3 Dot Mental Model" has been forever altered. If you see this exercise in the future, you will respond to it differently. From now on, the meaning of the 3 dots will be different for you.

In Your Mind-brain, *Meaning* Is Everything

The meaning of everything in your life is the result of mental models. Your mental models control your beliefs, attitudes and perceptions. They control the expectations you have for certain out-comes in your life and your response or reaction in any given situation. The way you're sitting right now, your posture, your reading speed and style, the way you're dressed, the style of your hair; all of these are the result of mental models. And perhaps most important to our discussion in this appendix, all of your habits flow from the mental models you have repeatedly activated during your lifetime.

Whether you are conscious of it or not, mental models are always active in your mind-brain, dictating your perceptions and determining the content and quality of every aspect of your life. The meaning of everything around you is determined by the mental models you have formed over your lifetime.

Learning to Drive a Stick Shift

The various connections in a mental model determine the meaning that is triggered when that mental model is accessed. For example, imagine learning to drive a stick shift and the connections your mind-brain forms in that mental model: coordinating the right hand on the gearshift, left hand on the steering wheel, left foot on the clutch, right foot on the brake and gas pedal. Add to this, feelings of embarrassment and awkwardness, and you have some of the initial connections in your mental model for "driving a stick shift." The mental model might look something like this:

"Driving a Stick-Shift"

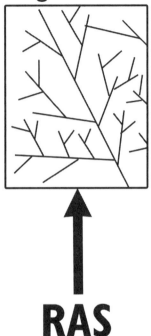

RAS

Now imagine while trying to coordinate the shifting procedure, you take your eyes off the road resulting in a horrible accident. You nearly die and you're in the hospital for 6 months. Imagine the vast number of connections added to your mental model for driving a stick-shift! Your transformed mental model would look something like this:

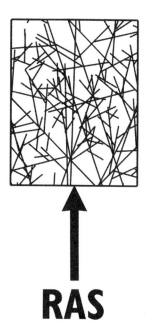

RAS

Imagine after your recovery, you get into a car with a manual transmission. As you take hold of the gearshift, imagine the mental model your RAS accesses and the vast array of connections that switch on. What does taking hold of that gearshift mean to you now? How is the meaning different from what it was before your accident?

Mental models with connections to powerful feelings, emotions, and memories, can create powerful thoughts, reactions, attitudes and habits. These mental models create powerful meaning.

Repetition and Mental Models

In addition to meaning, repetition also plays a major role in the power of mental models. The more a mental model is accessed and activated over time, the more powerful it becomes—its connections increase in number and strength. In addition, the pathway from the RAS to the mental model becomes increasingly rutted. This is akin to the saying; "Practice makes perfect." Doing the same thing over and over again forms powerful habits, bringing the activity or behavior to the point where you don't have to consciously think about it any more. Remember, your mind-brain's number one goal is efficiency. As soon as an activity becomes automatic, your mind-brain can move on and direct its energies and resources to learning and mastering something new.

When you first form a mental model, the pathway from your RAS is shallow and faint. It looks something like this:

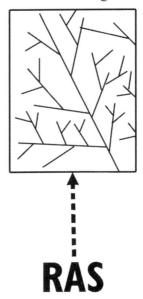

However, when you repeatedly access a specific mental model over time, an exaggerated pathway from your RAS to that mental model is formed; like a set of deeply rutted tire tracks on a muddy mountain road that has been traveled over and over again. In addition, each time a mental model is accessed, it expands—its connections increase in number and in strength.

RAS

When these dominant connections and deeply rutted pathway are present, your RAS will automatically select this mental model in the applicable situation.

Combining Meaning and Repetition = Powerful Habits

While meaning or repetition alone can form strong habits, putting the two together is a powerful combination. Consider the following real-life examples:

The Dentist and Vomit

I know a dentist whose greatest fear in life is throwing up—he fears it worse than death. (Imagine the vast connections in his mental model and the rutted pathway leading to it!) Early one morning as he approached his first patient of the day, he noticed something in the sink next to her. You guessed it—vomit! He thought, "Oh no, she got up late, ate too fast and was nervous about the visit. She's gone and thrown up in my sink!"

Even though he was 20 feet from the sink, he could smell it. Immediately he began to feel nauseous, his head started to hurt, and he was just about to stagger off to the restroom, when his assistant took the vomit from the sink and threw it across the room, bouncing it off his chest! It was rubber!

Knowing of his phobia, his assistant had purchased fake vomit at a gag shop and in collaboration with the patient, played a joke on him.

How is it that a grown man, an intelligent, successful professional, could "smell" plastic vomit? The answer: Meaning!

When the image of that vomit was routed through his RAS, where did the RAS instantly send it? Right down the rutted pathway to his dominant mental model for "vomit." All of the connections in that mental model, including those linked to his childhood flu memories, his smell, his stomach, his head, were instantly switched on like Las Vegas at night!

The Swastika

When Ruth was a child, she was separated from her parents and confined to a Nazi concentration camp. Although she survived the experience, the mental model (meaning) she formed through the horror and atrocities was vast and deep; accessed and expanded (repetition) thousands of times during her years of imprisonment.

Over 60 years later, as Ruth was walking down an American street, she instantly recognized the symbol on a flag hanging from an apartment balcony; it was the Swastika! When that image entered through her eyes and reached her RAS, it was immediately routed to its mental model. Imagine the deeply rutted pathway leading to the dominant mental model associated with that symbol and the meaning it had for Ruth!

Instantly Ruth experienced an overwhelming response in her mind-brain. Her heart rate spiked. Her breathing became heavy. All of the horror, fear, anger and myriad other emotions boiled up inside her. She started to cry as she felt panic racing through her. She felt an overwhelming urge to run! She was re-living the childhood trauma. As a result of the mental model, her mind-brain repeated the same physiological and biological responses it had produced countless times in the concentration camps.

A moment later, a child on a tricycle rode past her and looked up at the same flag. He showed no response to the image.

Why the extreme contrast in their reactions? The information they received through their eyes was identical. It was the meaning the image held for each one, the pre-existing mental models that were radically different. In the concentration camps Ruth had developed a powerful "Swastika mental model" and through accessing that mental model thousands of times, she had etched vast connections and a deeply rutted pathway leading to it. The habit (mental model) was still with her 60 years later.

Giving Blood

During his teenage years, Dave became addicted to heroine. After tremendous struggle through several recovery programs, he was finally able to continue on and lead a normal life. However, there was one thing Dave would never be able to do: give blood.

Just seeing the needle moving toward his vein caused a chemical and physiological reaction so powerful, it was as if heroine had just been injected into Dave's body! Frequent repetition of his earlier heroine habit had created a dominant mental model, meaning, and a rutted pathway that made the routine act of giving blood unbearable.

Reality vs. Memory

In the three examples above, you will notice that each of the individuals responded, not based on reality, but according to their perception of that reality; their memories; their pre-existing dominant mental models: The dentist could smell plastic vomit; Ruth saw the Nazi flag and reacted as if she were in immediate and terrible danger; Dave saw the needle and responded as if he had just injected cocaine.

I was recently in a 3-D movie where a cartoon character on a hover craft came straight at me and broke through a neon sign, sending shattering glass toward my face. Instinctively I threw my head back and almost broke the nose of the man sitting behind me!

Every day we react to people, situations and stimuli in ways that don't agree with reality. Why? Carefully consider the following principle:

When meaning is powerful, your mind-brain cannot distinguish between what is real and what your mental models tell you is real.

When a specific mental model is accessed over and over again in response to a certain stimulus or event, the response becomes habitual—it generates a habit. When confronted with the same circumstance or stimulus in the future, your mind-brain accesses the same mental model, producing the same response. Your mind-brain doesn't stop to ask, "Is this real or imagined?" As Page Bailey so eloquently states:

The mind-brain is always engaged in the process of bringing our experience into a state of agreement with the expectations that are produced by our mental models.

With dominant mental models and their resulting habits, history continually repeats itself in your mind-brain.

Are there automatic negative behaviors you keep repeating in your life that prevent you from attaining all the success, fulfillment and happiness you desire? Do you sometimes react in ways that aren't logical or based on reality? Do you have certain negative mental models with deeply rutted pathways that dominant your life? For example:

—Poor eating habits   —Negative financial habits

—Addictions   —Poor physical condition

—Negative thinking   —Unhappy marriage

—Critical or judgmental   —Unfulfilling career

—Temper   —Stressed out

—Fears or phobias   —Stuck in a rut

—Closed-minded, stubborn   —Childhood trauma

—Harboring a grudge or resentment —Cynical, pessimistic

If any of the above, or other negative patterns apply to you, it probably isn't for lack of effort. You probably have set numerous goals and tried many times to change negative habits and behaviors; sometimes succeeding and many times not. Why not? Because it's an unfair **competition**.

Habits vs. Goals: A Competition

Have you ever read a great idea in a self-improvement book, listened to a rousing sermon or speech, received a powerful desire or sudden impression to change something in your life? You try to implement it, but after a few days or weeks the excitement or determination fades and you're right back in your old habit. What happened?

Whenever you pursue a goal to behave differently than you have in the past, you immediately create a competition between your new goal and your existing dominant mental model.

Consider the following illustration:

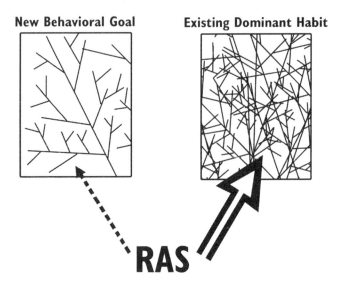

184

Notice the connections in the new mental model are few, while the connections in the dominant mental model are vast—the power of emotion and meaning in each mental model is very different. Notice the pathway leading to the mental model for the new behavioral goal is faint, while the pathway to the existing mental model/habit is deeply rutted.

Imagine each mental model is a magnet and your RAS is a compass arrow. The more powerful the connections in the mental model (feelings, emotions, memories—"meaning") the more powerful the magnetic force pulling your RAS toward that mental model. And, the more deeply rutted and well-traveled the pathway to that mental model, the more easily your RAS goes there.

What chance is there that your RAS will select the faint path to the mental model with few connections, over the deeply rutted path to the dominant mental model containing vast connections and powerful meaning? Without your conscious intervention, there's no chance. If you don't know how to use specific intervention tools in this automatic mind-brain process, expecting the new behavioral goal to win out is like facing a fire hose with a squirt gun.

In any given situation, the time it takes your RAS to select a mental model is a fraction of a second. And the entire selection process typically takes place at the unconscious level. You don't fully realize what's happening until the heat of the moment passes. Frustration and disappointment set in. You can't believe you've repeated the negative behavior again.

Based on what you now know about mental models and habits, and how they become dominant, is it reasonable to expect that just because

185

you read a few books and attended a seminar, you can derail a lifetime of mental model and habit formation?

Everyday people pit new behavioral goals against existing dominant habits. Not understanding that the mind-brain jealously guards its habits and doesn't change them quickly or easily, people attempt to change years of habitual behavior by reading a book, listening to a CD or attending a seminar. They attempt to reverse poor financial habits and get out of debt, reduce stress, improve a struggling marriage, lose weight and get into shape, break out of depression, balance a hectic life, overcome addictions. But aside from occasional victories, old habits seem to win out most of the time.

Are You Free to Choose?

You may be wondering, "Do I truly have the freedom to choose my own destiny or am I more or less subject to my negative habits and the dominant mental models that drive them?"

For centuries the debate of "free will" vs. "a product of my past" has raged in the scientific and philosophical communities.

My Past Made Me Do It

Many neuroscientists and psychologists insist that the concept of *conscious mind* can be fully explained as "neurons doing their electrochemical thing in the brain"—feelings, memory, attention, and free will are nothing more than neurochemical reactions over which we have no control. They claim there is no such thing as free will or independent thought, that these ideas are romantic illusions. Everything we have experienced over a lifetime is stored in the brain, thus their reasoning that every conscious thought we have can only be the result of that stored past. This group believes there is a specific place in the brain that directs every state of consciousness. If you apply a mild electrical shock to a particular location in the brain, the individual feels hunger, another spot and he feels fear, another conjures up memories of family. Once every brain location and matching function/emotion is traced, this group believes the mystery of the mind will be solved once and for all. As one neuroscientist involved in mapping all of the brain's functions put it "The mind is obsolete."

Sigmund Freud supported this theory. In his view, your present experience is fully determined by your past. The popular comedian Flip Wilson summarized many of Freud's theories with his mantra "The devil made me do it." If you replace the words "the devil" with "my past" then you are in one of the primary fields of Freud's speculative psychology. It is fascinating to note that in all of Freud's vast collected works—his books, papers and written lectures—there is not one use of the word *responsibility* or any other word that represents the concept of a person having true independent free will or the ability to respond in any way they choose.

The Power of Your Mind-brain and Your Will

The opposing view of many prominent neuroscientists and neuro-psychologists is that through the exercise of our mind, we can exert a literal force over the creation and transformation of presently active mental models in the physical brain, and the habits that their repeated use has created. This group readily acknowledges that while many of the mind-brain's functions are automatic and unconscious, we do have the power to consciously direct the things that truly matter in our lives. There is a powerful communication between the mind and the brain—what Dr. Page Bailey and others call the *mind-brain dialogue*. When we learn how to direct their dialogue, we can literally direct the formation of specific mental models in the physical brain. If we choose to, we can be the captain of our ship and determine our own destiny. This group believes that we can use the power of our will to override old dominant habits, and create new ones. Through the power of your will you can choose to modify the effects of your past, and create the future you desire. You are not a slave or a victim to *any* aspect of your past life.

Which group is right? Are you simply a product of your past or can you exercise your free will to truly change your life? Are you *response-able*? Do you have the ability to respond as you choose?

You Do Have Free Will and Choice!

Fortunately, those who claim our future can only be dictated by our past; that the brain controls everything in our lives, have been and are continuing to be proven wrong by cutting-edge mind-brain science. You do have free will. You can break out of old habits! You can modify the effects of your past and create a future that you desire.

In the 1980s and '90s, the brilliant and courageous research and work of professionals like Candace Pert, Antonio Damasio, Jeffrey Schwartz, John Hughes, Hans Kosterlitz, Page Bailey, Francis Schmitt, Gerald Edelman and others began to shatter many of the cherished beliefs held by Western scientists and psychologists for more than three centuries. These pioneers proved that the body is not a mindless machine; simply obeying the dictates of the brain. There is a mind and it directs both the brain and the body. Each of us can use the power of our mind to direct and improve our future, without fear of our past habits, environments or family history.

Yet, there are many in our society who choose to live their lives on autopilot, allowing existing mental models, dominant habits, and their past to dictate their future. For these individuals, the claim that "the power of the mind is a romantic illusion" holds true. Concerning these individuals, Dr. Jeffrey Schwartz in his ground-breaking book, *The Mind and The Brain*, states:

For if we truly believe, when the day is done, that our mind and all that term entails—the choices we make, the reactions we have, the emotions we feel—are nothing but the expressions of a machine governed by the rules of classical physics and chemistry, and that our behavior follows ineluctably from the working of our neurons, then we're forced to conclude that the subjective sense of freedom is a user illusion.

The bottom line is you get to choose! You can live your life on autopilot at the unconscious level, or you can learn to consciously exercise the power of your mind to overcome your past and direct your future.

Your Conscious and Unconscious Experience

If you truly desire to overcome past negative habits and dominant mental models, and form new ones leading to the realization of your highest goals and aspirations, then you must learn to bring your habit formation process to the conscious level.

The processes in your body (including your brain) operate at two levels: The level of which you are aware (conscious) and that of which you are not aware (unconscious).

Most of the activity in your body place at the unconscious level; billions of cellular processes taking place continuously. However, unconscious activity is not limited to functions such as digestion, immune system processes, blood flow and breathing. Many of your behaviors, beliefs and attitudes have become so habitual, their mental models so dominant, that you are no longer aware of the process. You can remain stuck in your day-to-day ruts, repeating the same behaviors over and over again unaware of the processes going on below the surface.

Compared to all the unconscious activity going on inside of us, that of which we become consciously aware is very small. Page Bailey uses an analogy of the vast ocean to represent our unconscious experience, and a tiny teacup of salt water, our conscious experience.

But here is the grand key: You can use the power of your will at the conscious level to dictate much of what goes on at the unconscious level—the tiny teacup can influence the vast ocean! Your mind-brain is designed to give you a choice!

Consider what Candace Pert said about this reality in her revolutionary book, *Molecules of Emotion*:

While much of the activity of the body, according to the new information model, does take place at the automatic, unconscious level, what makes this model so different is that it can explain how it is also possible for our conscious mind to enter the network and play a deliberate part.

Of all the billions of activities going on in your body when one suddenly reaches your awareness, your consciousness, it is so special and unique that Page Bailey refers to it as privileged information—information that has reached the *Privileged Place*. It is only in the Privileged Place that you can exercise your will to eliminate past negative habits and develop new positive behaviors.

The Power of the Privileged Place

To better understand the Privileged Place, consider the following expansion of Page Bailey's analogy of the ocean:

Imagine you're standing on the shore looking out over the vast ocean. You can't see the billions of activities going on under the surface; they are invisible to you. This represents your unconscious experience or that of which you are not aware. Many people live significant portions of their lives at very low levels of conscious awareness, "below the surface of the water," allowing themselves to be driven by their past: family background, childhood traumas, negative habits, attitudes and routines; like passive backseat passengers in a car forever traveling down the same deeply rutted road. Unknowingly, they continually add to this cycle through self-talk, TV and other media, input from family and friends, repeating unproductive behaviors again and again, etc. A recent news article stated the following:

"Recent studies conducted by a Stanford University research team have revealed that 'what we watch' does have an effect on our imaginations, our learning patterns, and our behaviors. First, we are exposed to new behaviors and characters. Next, we learn or acquire these new behaviors [form mental models]. The last and most crucial step is that we adopt these behaviors as our own [they become a habit]. One of the most critical aspects of human development that we need to understand is the influence of 'repeated viewing' and 'repeated verbalizing' [repetition] in shaping our [mental models]. The information goes in, 'harmlessly, almost unnoticed,' on a daily basis, but we don't react to it until later, when we aren't able to realize the basis for our reactions [a habit has formed at the unconscious level]. In other words, our value system is being formed without any conscious awareness on our part of what is happening."

People who allow themselves to passively form mental models and habits in this way, repeat saying such as: (1) "You can't change the past," (2) "That's just the way I am," (3) "Learn to live with it. We're too old to change things now."

For these individuals, much of life is an unconscious experience driven by habitual processes they are unaware of. Their RAS activates the same mental models over and over again. They are stuck in the same old behavioral cycle or rut. Page Bailey calls this *living a circular life*:

Circular Life

In a circular life, you live as a slave to existing dominant habits and unproductive behaviors, a product of your past. In the confines of the circle, your options are extremely limited.

Now imagine as you're looking out over the ocean, your attention is suddenly drawn to an object breaking through the surface. This represents activity that has appeared at the conscious level. Page calls this experience *privileged*. He describes people having conscious experience and learning how to use that conscious experience as entering the Privileged Place. Conscious experience is privileged experience because you can do something with it, something about it, and something to it. Only privileged information—that of which we become aware—is information we can use to build habits with acts of our will that enable us to achieve the new goals that bring us to a place of greater success and happiness.

The grand key to getting what you want in your life and your relationships is learning how to bring your habit formation process into this Privileged Place where you can direct it. It is only in this Privileged Place where you can permanently form the positive habits you desire, and eliminate the negative habits that you no longer desire to be present in your life. You can learn how to take something you're already great at—forming habits (also known as *Successability)*—and in the Privileged Place use this process to purposefully and consciously sit in the driver's seat on your journey to your ideal self and your ideal life.

Direct the Formation of Mental Models and Habits

While you genetically inherit your tendency to build mental models and habits, you do not inherit the specific mental models and habits themselves. You can choose and direct the mental models you build and the habits that flow from them. You have been building mental models your entire life. Most of the time you have been doing this at the unconscious level. Many of your mental models were built as a result of the environment you grew up in and your family of origin. Many came from experiences you had no control over, while others you purposely directed.

The point is, you are already amazingly effective and efficient at forming mental models and habits; this is the built-in natural tendency or *Successability* of your mind-brain. While most self-improvement programs, marriage handbooks, weight-loss regimes and money-making strategies contain valuable information and great ideas, they fail to give people easy-to-implement tools they can use daily to enter the Privileged Place and consciously direct the natural mental model and habit-forming processes already built into the mind-brain.

193

The definition of insanity is often stated as "doing the same thing over and over again while expecting a different result." You can't form new habits and achieve the successes you desire while continuing to access and utilize your existing negative mental models. You must build and access new mental models that match your goals for the future. You must break out of your circular life.

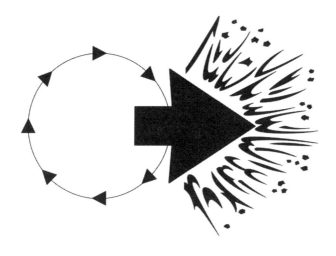

You can only do this in the Privileged Place. Consider the wonderful example of Dr. Jeffrey Schwartz and his OCD patients.

The Power of the Privileged Place: The Remarkable Success of OCD Patients

If there is any example of individuals living lives dominated by what goes on under the surface, by automatic behaviors, it is those who suffer from Obsessive Compulsive Disorder or OCD. OCD is a neuropsychiatric disease marked by distressing, intrusive, unwanted thoughts (the obsessive part) that trigger intensive urges to perform ritualistic behaviors (the compulsive part). OCD patients describe their obsessive thoughts as coming from a part of their mind that is not their true self, like a highjacker taking over their brain's controls. Thus the urge to wash their hands for the fortieth time, fully realizing that their hands aren't dirty, or ritualistically dialing a friend's phone number twenty seven times before finally letting the number ring through, knowing full well—despite the nagging in their gut—that failing to do so will not doom their friend to instant death.

Because the obsessive thoughts can't be silenced, the resulting compulsive behavior can't be resisted. OCD sufferers feel like puppets on the end of a string, manipulated and jerked around by a cruel pup-peteer—their own brain. These individuals are the ultimate example of someone enslaved by powerful mental models and automatic behaviors; individuals dominated by negative habits.

In the 1990s a brilliant and courageous psychiatrist, Dr. Jeffrey M. Schwartz began developing a revolutionary treatment for OCD that has forever changed the way we view our abilities to overcome nega-tive habits—to change the effects of our past. For over a decade Dr. Schwartz worked with OCD patients helping them achieve miraculous results, far beyond traditional methods and what was believed possible. Dr. Schwartz made the amazing discovery that willfully directing one's conscious thoughts (in the Privileged Place) produces a mental energy, a force that causes the mind-brain to literally shrink existing dominant mental models, and build and expand new healthy ones! This mental force actually "vetoes" the RAS's natural tendency to select the dominant mental model and literally moves it to access the newly desired mental model!

Dr. Schwartz refers to this as "Free Will" vs. "Free Won't" — I "will" cause my RAS to direct energy to new healthy mental models, and I "won't" allow the old negative mental models to rule my life. By bringing their automatic OCD behaviors above the surface into the conscious Privileged Place, his patients were able to use their own mental force to literally change the physical structure and circuitry of their brains and attain a whole new life! These remarkable results, and similar success with Taurette's Syndrome, Chronic Depression and other disorders are documented in Jeffrey's astonishing book, *The Mind and The Brain: Neuroplasticity and the Power of Mental Force*.

Consider the "before and after" mind-brain processes and brain structure/circuitry of the OCD patients:

Illustration 1: Before working with Dr. Schwartz, the OCD patients' mental model process took place at the unconscious level where they were helpless to do anything about it. The RAS followed its natural tendency and selected the dominant OCD mental model every time. The OCD patients remained stuck in their rut; in their circular life.

197

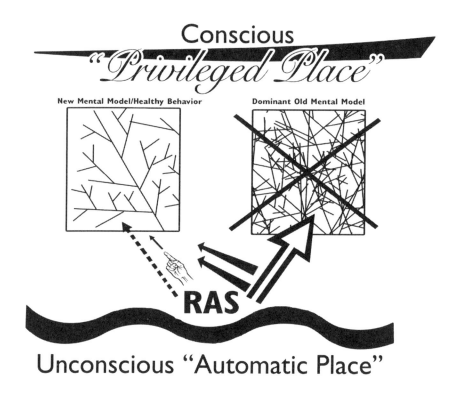

Conscious
"Privileged Place"

New Mental Model/Healthy Behavior **Dominant Old Mental Model**

RAS

Unconscious "Automatic Place"

Illustration #2: Under Dr. Schwartz's program, OCD patients' were taught to bring the mental model process above the surface into the Privileged Place where they could direct it. Through the exercise of their free will, the patients held an image of their new behavioral goal in their conscious thoughts until the mental force needed to move their RAS to the new mental model was created. Even though the pathway to the new mental model was faint, the connections few, they actually "vetoed" their RAS's natural tendency to select the dominant mental model. Mental energy created a tangible force that made the RAS switch to the new mental model for healthy behavior.

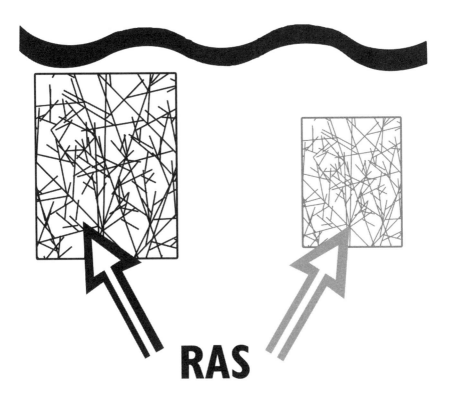

Illustration #3: With practice and repetition over time, the new mental model became dominant while the old OCD mental model faded. Eventually, the entire process became automatic, the new healthy behavior a habit, and was moved "under the surface" where the OCD patients no longer had to think about it. They were free to move on and accomplish higher goals and aspirations in their lives!

In parallel but separate professional work, Dr. Page Bailey has developed his own unique neuropsychological and mind-brain therapy programs. For nearly 20 years Page has been using his powerful techniques to help his clients recover from chronic illnesses, chronic pain, addictions of all types, depression, sleep disorders, and many other kinds of mental and physical disorders.

This Program is for Everyone

You may be wondering, "What do OCD sufferers and people with serious disorders have to do with my current situation and goals for the future?" The purpose in citing these examples is not to suggest that the *LifeBalance System* with its *3 Rules* and *3 Tools* is only designed for people with serious disorders and challenges. The work of Jeffrey Schwartz, Page Bailey and others is sited to illustrate the enormous power of this program for everyone, regardless of their situation, needs or goals for the future. The LifeBalance System has helped thousands of individuals achieve success in every area of their lives. With amazing results being experienced by people with extreme challenges, imagine what you can do to overcome your own negative habits and move forward to attain the success, joy and fulfillment you desire!

ATTENTION!
Entering
the
Privileged Place.
PROCEED
WITH
CAUTION

Attention! Entering the Privileged Place

As Dr. Schwartz, Dr. Bailey and others have clearly shown, the Privileged Place is a place of power! Thoughts are things—tangible, traceable, producing a mental force that acts on the physical brain and body. What this means in real-life application, is that you get what you think about; you get what you expect. The thoughts you allow to play on the stage of your mind create a self-fulfilling prophecy; good or bad—you choose the mental models that are activated by the thoughts you entertain.

Many people allow whatever thoughts happen to enter the Privileged Place to dwell there, generating a mental force and the resulting consequences. Too often, these thoughts are negative, based on years of habit. They rise up from below the surface and enter the Privileged Place, generating the same negative behaviors they always have. Herb Otto, a national expert on human potential, made an interesting observation. He claimed that only one out of every 110 people concentrated on their positive attributes. The other 109 (or over 99% of us) tend to

201

focus on our flaws and failures. Most of us become preoccupied with what does not go well rather than what does.

Guard well the gates to your Privileged Place, the place of your conscious thoughts. It is a place of incredible power. Whatever you allow to enter and dwell in this sacred place will fully determine the quality and success of every aspect of your life.

Harnessing and Directing Your Habit Formation Powers

As already mentioned, each of us is incredibly effective and efficient at forming habits—we've been doing it since the day of our birth. Most of our habits are formed at the unconscious level, without our being aware of the process. Unfortunately, some of these habits, beliefs, thoughts and behavior patterns are negative, disruptive and keep us from all the success and happiness we desire in our lives and relationships. But here is the good news:

The same steps you have followed to form your negative habits can be used to form positive habits and achieve the success and happiness you desire in your life and relationships. The process is the same. You're already great at it! You already have a natural built-in *Success-ability.* All you need are a few simple rules and basic tools to bring the process in the Privileged Place and direct it.

The process of combining 30+ years of coaching individuals in the LifeBalance System, with the cutting-edge work in neuropsychology and clinical psychology carried out by Jeffrey Schwartz, Page Bailey and others, provides for us the *3 Rules for building new mental models and habits.* The *3 Rules*, and the *3 Tools* that accompany them, will provide you with a simple daily system for entering the Privileged Place and using the power of your will to create the mental force necessary to direct the creation and transformation of your mental models and habits.

The Three Rules and Three Tools will allow you to create what are known as *Consciously Directed Goals*: goals you bring into the Privileged Place on a daily basis where you can direct their progress and fulfillment. Consciously Directed Goals shine in stark contrast to their distant cousins: the written goal in the day planner; the New Year's Resolution; and the "this is finally it" declaration of a determination to change. These "good intentions" often fail, because they fail to incorporate the *3 Rules of Mental Model and Habit Creation and Transformation* that are essential to creating Consciously Directed Goals.

The 3 Rules of Mental Model/Habit Creation/Transformation and Consciously Directed Goals

Each of the three rules that follow are preceded by their equivalent negative habit-formation principle. Compare the automatic "unconscious" habit-formation process you've been engaged in all your life, with the "Privileged Place" process of Consciously Directed Goals.

Negative Habit-Formation Principle #1: Over your lifetime you have formed negative mental models with vast connections to feelings, emotions and memories, producing deep and powerful meaning. These connections are like a magnetic force attracting the compass needle of your RAS. It's no surprise that these dominant mental models are easily and automatically selected by your RAS.

Rule #1: Clearly state your goal and motive in a way that accesses *mental models* with powerful *meaning*.

The negative habits, beliefs and behaviors in our lives stem from mental models with powerful meaning. In order to form new positive habits, you must first build mental models with equally powerful connections, emotions and meaning. Control meaning and you control your future. The most effective way to do this is to incorporate four basic elements into the description of each of your Consciously Directed Goals:

1. **Clearly State Your Goal:** This may appear to be obvious—scarcely worth mentioning, but many people are far too broad and generic in describing their goals. Common are statements like: "I want to make more money." "I want to improve my marriage." "I want to get into shape." "I want to lose weight." These generic statements make it difficult for the mind-brain to build a specific mental model to match the desired goal.

    Imagine you have written down your goal and a complete stranger reads it. From your written description alone, would the person understand the specifics of your goal? Look at your goal statement and ask yourself, "What do I mean by that?" Keep refining and asking that question until you can refine no further. Now you have a clearly stated goal.

2. **Motive:** Identify and clearly state your motive—"why" you want to achieve the specific goal; its positive benefits, rewards and outcomes. Doing this creates three critical results in the mental model formation process: (a) A powerful motive forms powerful connections and meaning in the desired mental model; (b)

Focusing on motive initiates and magnifies the mental force that moves your RAS to select the new mental model over the old dominant one; (c) When faced with obstacles and the temptation to fall back into your old habit, turning your mindful attention to your motive will instantly activate the desired mental model.

3.   **Act As If:** Visualize yourself already having achieved your goal. Describe in great detail how you feel. Describe what it has done for the quality of your life, relationships, your successes, etc. Describe how those you care about respond positively to the achievement of your goal. Imagine the vast connections this forms in the mental model you are building.

In a recent lecture, Dr. Antonio Damasio, one of the world's leading neuroscientists, taught that the mind-brain forms memories, not only based on past experiences, but also based on the future that we expect. Thus, as we expect and visualize the achievement of a specific goal, we build mental models with memories of that expected future—connections to all of the images, feelings and emotions associated with that future. Thus, you can build powerful new mental models with vast connections based on your desired future—as if it were already a reality! Remember; when meaning is powerful, your mind-brain cannot distinguish between what is real and what your mental models tell you is real.

4.   **Present Tense:** One of the most effective ways to create powerful meaning in your mind-brain is to express an expectation. The final element under Rule #1 is to state your goal, your motive and your visualization of its realization in the present tense—as if all of

it is already taking place, already a reality. Rather than using statements like, "I will . . . ," "I want . . . ," or "I try to . . . ," put everything in the present tense: "I am . . . ," "I do . . . ," "I deserve . . . ," "I am becoming . . . ," "I feel . . ."

Remember, your mind-brain is always in the process of bringing your experience into a state of agreement with your expectation. Based on what you expect or believe, your mind-brain activates the mental model most suited to making that expectation a reality.

Negative Habit-Formation Principle #2: Negative thought patterns, behaviors and habits are repeated and practiced thousands of times—expanding and reinforcing the mental models they flow from. This is why the pathways leading to these mental models become so deeply rutted.

Rule #2: Engage in Daily Practice and Repetition in the Privileged Place

Many of your dominant mental models and habits have been created, accessed and expanded over many years of daily practice and repetition. You must find a simple, easy way to generate the same type of daily practice and repetition if your new mental models and habits are to become dominant. On a consistent daily basis, you need to bring your Consciously Directed Goals into the Privileged Place and begin forming increasingly rutted pathways to new mental models. Through this daily repetition, your RAS will begin activating your desired mental models automatically—you will form new habits. Each time the desired mental model is accessed, it expands; its connections grow in number and strength. Each time the old dominant mental model is not selected, it shrinks and the pathway to it becomes increasingly faint.

In *The Mind and The Brain*, Dr. Jeffrey Schwartz sites a study directed by neuroscientist Alvaro Pascual-Leone. Pascual-Leone had one group of volunteers practice a five-finger piano exercise, and a comparable group merely think about practicing it. They visualized each finger movement, playing the piece in their heads one note at a time. Brain scans of the physical practice group showed changes in brain structure as expected. But amazingly the same level of brain change was noted in the mental rehearsal group! Merely thinking about moving one's fingers produced brain changes comparable to actually moving them.

Simply visualizing or "mentally practicing" your desired goals begins creating mental models and habits leading to their fulfillment.

Eventually you can move the process to the unconscious level where you don't have to think about it any more and you can shift your willful attention to other Consciously Directed Goals you want to achieve. Your life becomes one of success building on success, a perpetual upward spiral.

Negative Habit-Formation Principle #3: Unfortunately, negative habits don't require any accountability to form and continue progressing. Because these habits are typically created and reinforced at the unconscious level, the process is "automatic."

Rule #3: Give Yourself and Others Permission to Hold You Accountable

In the hectic busyness and stress of everyday life it's very easy to lose conscious awareness of your Consciously Directed Goals and slip below the surface, back into old habits You need to give yourself and special people in your life permission to remind you and hold you accountable to consistently implement daily tools for the creation, transformation and continual development of new habits.

Important Note: In the previous chapters of this book, you were introduced to 3 Basic Tools that make it easy for you to fully implement into your daily life all components of the three essential rules described above. You will take full control of the mental model and habit formation processes and begin your journey toward your ideal self and your ideal life.

Moving to Ever Higher Levels

Through the daily implementation of the LifeBalance System, you can continuously bring the areas of your life that you want to change, or the goals you want to achieve, into the Privileged Place. Here you can use your natural built-in Successability to make your desired behaviors automatic and your goals a reality. You can then move on to the next level and do the same thing. Your life will look something like this:

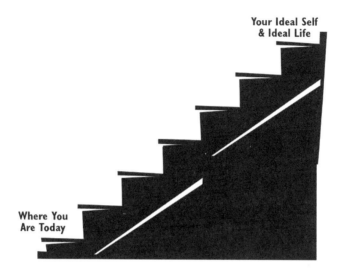

Through the remarkable power of directing your mind-brain in the Privileged Place, the exercise of your free will, you truly can overcome every negative habit and achieve your highest goals and aspirations. Page Bailey summed up the entire process described in this chapter in a single paragraph. He once described this paragraph as "A single statement summary of my life's work."

I have studied and pondered this paragraph many times and each time I do I learn something new. I invite you to ponder its meaning and application in your own life. And as you do, I invite you learn, embrace and fully implement the LifeBalance System in your daily life to turn your dreams into reality.

Dr. Page Bailey
The Brain-Mind Dialogue

"The mind is the modified history of that which the brain has experienced. The history of brain experience is a living and active record of our lives. The brain in its dialogue with the mind does not give us a personal history that is written in stone. That dialogue provides us with a malleable history that has been and that is being continually remade by both our dominant present purposes and the specific behavioral goals toward which our creative energies are now being directed."

As you progress through the LifeBalance System, developing 2, 3, 4 or more editions of your LifeCreed we encourage you to review this appendix occasionally. Points or concepts that may have slipped by you will now take on new meaning as you have more experience, and move to higher levels of awareness and achievement.

Special Note: Does all the information in this Appendix mean to suggest that the mentally ill, the addict, the violent husband, the suicidal teenager only need to exercise their will to correct the problem—they only remain sick because of a lack of will power? To approach these challenges as an all-or-nothing-choice or no-choice is far too simplistic.

There are situations where years of dominant mental model access and reinforcement at the unconscious level creates a habit so powerful, it can become overwhelming. Sometimes unwanted negative processes at the unconscious and conscious levels are too great for mental force to overcome. Sometimes will power alone isn't enough, but must be

210

accompanied by knowledge, training, support from loved ones and the community, and appropriate medical, psychological and therapeutic interventions. The LifeBalance System, its rules and tools, are designed to work in harmony with and support higher level interventions when needed.

First-Person, Present-Tense Phrases

I am pure energy and I . . .

I am strong when I . . .

I am strong and able to . . .

I am strong and self-reliant in . . .

I am successful at . . .

Each day I am becoming more . . .

I am unique because I . . .

I am wealthy and . . .

I attract money from . . .

I attract success because I . . .

I create the environment where I can . . .

I begin again to . . .

I believe in myself and my ability to . . .

I breathe deeply when . . .

I buy only healthy foods

I can do it because . . .

I control what I eat because . . .

I deserve good things

I deserve money

I deserve success

I deserve the good life

I do it

I do it easily

I do it for me

I do it now

I do it today

I do one thing at a time

I eat right

I enjoy success

I enjoy exercise

I exercise everyday

I feel fantastic when I . . .

Daily I am progressing toward . . .

I love . . .

I realize . . .

I go . . .

I treasure . . .

213

I work toward . . .

I search for . . .

I am . . .

My mind is open

My strength is multiplied when I . . .

My will moves mountains

I hold my head high and I . . .

I am satisfied with smaller portions

I am successful

I like myself

I love myself

I move lightly when I . . .

I practice . . .

I read food labels because . . .

I relax when . . .

I relax and enjoy eating less

I remember _____ easily

I remember _____ vividly

I rise above all obstacles

I smile when . . .

I speak up when . . .

I stick to it easily, naturally

I succeed because . . .

I succeed again and again at . . .

I take action now

I feel at peace

I only eat fresh, natural foods

I follow my instincts

I follow success

I have concentrated my will on . . .

I have energy and enthusiasm

I keep an open mind

I let go of . . .

I have . . .

I commit myself to . . .

I focus on . . .

I lead others to . . .

I hold . . .

I seek . . .

LifeCreed Samples

ATTENTION: Do not review these sample LifeCreeds until after you have answered the LifeCreed questions in Chapter 12.

LifeCreed Excerpts

These are excerpts from the actual LifeCreeds of some of my clients. Having completed your initial LifeCreed statements, you know something of what it takes to create a LifeCreed: the effort, the soul-searching, the expression of your deepest feelings, dreams and ideals. I'm grateful to my clients for their willingness to share excerpts from their private LifeCreeds with you.

Remember: These excerpts reflect the ideal self and ideal life my clients were striving for. Many of these ideals were not yet realized when the Creeds were written.

My Relationship with my Creator

Sample Creed Excerpts #1: Spiritual
(This excerpt is written like a prayer to God.)

Heavenly Father, I am a true disciple of Christ and strive to emulate his example. I want to be like Him and serve people as He did. I start every day at 6:00 A.M. by talking with you and I always ask for your help in overcoming my faults and in being more Christ-like. I strive to communicate with you all day long and listen carefully for your counsel. Since I desire to become more Christ-like, I study His example from the scriptures every day in my office from 7:30 to 8:00 A.M. As I am doing this I feel your spirit and I learn how to think and act more like my savior. This time brings me feelings of great peace, perspective and joy.

I know you love me, and I love you, and when I talk to you I feel that we are talking face to face. Because I love you I obey your commandments. I seek each day to understand the commandments and why you have given them. I strive to see the direction that obeying the commandments points me in, and I work harder to obey my understanding of "the higher law."

I magnify my Church participation by working with all my heart and soul when asked to help. I am not content to do what others have done but I study the assignment and apply my special talents of empathy and leadership to do more than is expected. I am striving to be worthy at all times to be guided by the Holy Spirit and I seek diligently and listen and obey all promptings. This helps me be a much better father, husband and servant to everyone around me.

I strive to treat all people equally. I seek those who have spiritual and physical needs. I help them because I see the face of the Savior in every individual. My greatest joy comes from serving others and I love it.

I lead my family by example. I am prepared for every Sunday. I assist all members of the family in their preparation and keep Sunday a relaxed, pleasant day. I spend all of Sunday seeking to serve my family and draw closer to them. My efforts on Sunday have a positive impact on my relationships with my family all week long.

I meet with my Sweetheart from 6:30 to 7:00 P.M. on Sundays to plan our week and to make certain that I am aware of any special events or needs in the family during the coming week.

Sample Creed Excerpt #2: Spiritual

I love searching the scriptures and other spiritual materials every morning at 7:30 for 20 minutes, seeking for what the Lord wants me to know and do to serve Him better. I have committed to Him that I read the scriptures every day without fail. I honor this commitment and doing so makes me feel good and brings me a rich outpouring of his spirit. I always spend one hour at 10:00 Saturday evenings reading and pondering Sunday School lessons so I can fully participate and contribute in church. It's very fulfilling and satisfying to join in the Sunday School discussions with my brothers and sisters.

I am a dynamic spiritual leader in my home. I lead by providing a positive example for my family by studying the scriptures, saying my personal prayers, and calling the family together for our family prayer every morning at 8:00 A.M. Through my example I invite the spirit into our home and this makes a positive difference in the peace and harmony that is there.

I love discussing my life every morning with God. I thank Him for all the blessings He has given me and I constantly strive to spend more time praying to improve our relationship to a deeper, more personal level. My relationship with Him is so vital that I love taking time to communicate my innermost feelings to Him all during the day

217

and evening. Doing this makes me more successful in every other part of my life.

I am mastering the habit of going to bed by 10:30 P.M. and I realize that this is the solution to the accomplishment of many of my spiritual goals.

I am the head of my family and I take the lead in our weekly Family Councils on Monday nights. I know the Lord smiles as He watches the way I lead out in my family

I am young, healthy and happy. I am complete. I am proud of my body and my face. I am gifted in body and mind. I overcome any obstacle. I am alive and aware. I am in control. Life is wonderful!

I am a caring person. I am sensitive and responsive to people's needs. I am expressive and loving. I create great friendships and loyalties because I give great love and loyalty.

I am intelligent and sensitive and love a good time. I have the ability to see humor and use my wit to soften life's stressful times. I am resilient and strong.

I love to dance and sing. I love adventure and excitement. Life is always a challenge and an opportunity. I seek to find the bright and hopeful side to every challenge.

I love peace and harmony in my home. I have an excellent relationship with Judy because I actively listen to her. At mealtime we always discuss her day; at bedtime I take time to listen to her prayers, and then I softly scratch her back to relax her. I am sensitive to her feelings. Bedtime is a special time for us to talk and listen to each other and review the day's events.

Judy is a joy to me, an inspiration. I ask Judy how I can be a better mom and I listen. I give wise counsel to my daughter. I have infinite patience. I respond to frustrating situations with calmness and serenity. I express my concerns with love.

I create an atmosphere of love and acceptance in my home. My child and her friends feel unconditional love and freedom to grow and develop their individual, unique gifts and personalities. Because I continually seek to be nonjudgmental and see the good in individuals, and because I use my sense of humor, my home often rings with laughter, abounding in warmth and love.

I create an atmosphere where Judy is taught and encouraged by example and word to have good manners and consideration for others' feelings. My actions always demand respect. I tolerate only loving and kind behavior. Everyone's space is of equal importance in my home.

I am consistent. I have the strength and ability to accomplish my goals. I am not alone. I need and accept God's help and love, and also the friendship and advice from those persons whose wisdom and experience exceed my own. Because I am intelligent and successful I welcome and appreciate the counsel of positive and successful people. I seek constant and continual encouragement and give the same. I align myself with the loving, positive, good powers and energies of the universe.

I am good and I respond to love—love of God, love for myself, and love for my fellowman. I am committed to my course.

I choose to do right and worship God in deed and thought. I give thanks for my blessings. I acknowledge the power and the authority of God and His servants. I am in His service and in His debt. I thank Him always, day and night.

219

My Relationship with Self: Emotional/Intellectual

Sample Creed #1: Emotional/Intellectual

I know that it is okay to say "No" or to say "I'm tired" or to even say "I don't want to" when someone asks me to do something. I stay in control of my time so that I am always stress-free and in full control of my emotions. I schedule my time carefully and keep the commitments which I have made. Doing this brings great peace into my life.

I listen to Charles Beckett's tape on communication between men and women in order to stay focused on the different methods of communicating and in order to deal objectively with other's responses to my requests or suggestions. I listen to these tapes on my drive to work and on my way home. I am improving my communication skills more each day and my family and co-workers are amazed at how effective I am. I create an atmosphere where people can feel comfortable and enjoy talking with me.

I schedule my time so that I have proper rest. I retire before 10:00 P.M. Sunday through Thursday and I arise rejuvenated and excited at 6:00 A.M. Monday through Friday mornings. I carefully monitor my medications and take my vitamins on a daily basis so that I have the physical reserves I need to maintain proper health.

I discuss problems promptly so that I do not harbor bad feelings toward others which could create emotional and spiritual stress on me. Others appreciate my openness and gentle honesty and this improves my relationships with those around me.

I remind myself daily that faith and fear cannot exist at the same time and that with proper communication with my Heavenly Father I do not REACT to fear as I make my decisions, but ACT out of knowledge and faith. Doing this increases my self-confidence and my confidence in God, knowing that together we can do anything!

I always remember the plaque in our bedroom that says "LORD, HELP ME TO REMEMBER TODAY THAT NOTHING IS GOING TO HAPPEN THAT YOU AND I TOGETHER CAN'T HANDLE." This is one of the first things I see each morning and it gives me a gentle reminder as to the power of prayer in my life and the blessing of peace to my soul.

I read articles on good mental health as I become aware of them, and I attend classes and workshops on stress and burnout at each convention I attend so that I am always alert to the need for emotional and mental fitness. When I learn something that is meaningful and important in my life, I put it in my LifeCreed where it becomes part of who I am.

Sample Creed #2: Emotional/Intellectual

I thrive on gaining new knowledge and learning new marketing ideas in my chosen career. I learn one new idea each day that improves my skills and effectiveness and I record that idea in my idea book. I review these ideas every Monday morning at 8:00 A.M. to refresh myself in all the new knowledge I have gained. I take the most important things I learn and put them in my Creed so I can listen to them everyday. After awhile they become automatic habits. By doing this I am constantly moving to a higher level in my career.

Every night at 9:30 P.M., I love reading from books of fiction and motivation. I am so excited to learn that I stay wide-awake and alert while reading. I have to pry myself away from books in order to go on to other important events. I listen to motivational tapes on Tuesdays and Thursdays while eating my lunch. When I hear something that really stands out I make a note of it and put it in my Creed. I am becoming more and more positive and balanced with each passing day.

I demonstrate my positive attitude about learning to my children and I create an atmosphere where they can develop the same enthusiasm for learning that I have.

Sample Creed #3: Emotional/Intellectual

My mind is focused! Every morning during my prayer and meditation period I plan my day, emphasizing the goals and objectives of my Creed. Then, throughout the day, as interruptions occur I handle them graciously and immediately return to the priority at hand. The intensity of my concentration impresses all who come in contact with me. I maintain focus!

I sense my capacity to remember things growing every day. As I meet a new person I find myself repeating his name over and over during the conversation and associating it with something unique about him. I am also using this tremendous skill to memorize one new poem or quote each week and find this is one of the most rewarding mental exercises I am involved in. People are amazed at my remarkable memory.

I always sing in the church choir, taking other opportunities to sing solo or with groups. I love seeing the happiness on people's faces when they listen to my music. This is a wonderfully fulfilling part of my life.

My love for music has also expanded to instruments. Each evening at 9:00 P.M. before we retire, uplifting music from the piano and French horn fills our home. I constantly work to create the atmosphere and give encouragement so that our family can sing and play instruments together often. My love for and involvement in music touches all the family for good.

I am a terrific speller. What used to be a weakness has become a great strength. I am amazed at how I use the spell-check less and less when I write letters and business documents.

I love reading! Truth expanding in the soul is one of life's most sublime experiences. As I read each morning during exercise, and on Tuesday and Thursday evenings at 8:00 P.M. during study time, my soul expands and it becomes an uplifting experience for me.

My Relationship with My Body: Health/Fitness

Sample Creed #1: Health/Fitness

Each day I become a more healthy person. Others can tell it because I look great. I have abundant energy because my body is extremely conditioned and very well maintained. I have so much stamina that others are amazed and have difficulty keeping up.

My physique is increasingly slender and well proportioned. I reach and maintain my ideal weight of 190 pounds by exercising six times a week (Monday to Saturday from 6:00 to 6:30 A.M.). My resting heart rate is 60 BPM. I ride my stationary bicycle for 18 minutes, perform flexibility and stretching exercises, and work out with light weights to keep my body firm and well conditioned. I make certain that I maintain a heart rate of 150 for at least 12 minutes during my exercise period so aerobically my heart stays in perfect condition. I always use the stairs and take them two at a time when there are only two or three flights, and I walk at least a mile Monday, Wednesday, and Friday. I encourage my sweetheart to walk with me. For short trips the car stays in the garage and I use my bicycle.

I enjoy life. And to ensure that I continue enjoying life, I take extreme care to eat well-prepared and nourishing meals. I eat three meals a day and delight in a variety of vegetables and grains, along with small amounts of meat. I get seven hours of sleep at night, because I go to bed at 11:00 P.M. I am up at 6:00 A.M. and I feel fabulous!

Sample Creed #2: Health/Fitness

I see myself weighing 199 pounds and I look and feel like a million bucks! My waist is 35 inches and my chest is as solid as a rock.

I get up at 5:30 A.M. to enjoy the most beautiful part of the day. I walk 3 miles every morning in 41 minutes which makes me feel like I am on top of the world. I know that I am in control.

I eat three well-balanced meals every day that consist of the right amount from each of the food groups. I have tons of energy and enough vitality to tackle all the activities of the day. I eat legal snacks in the evening and always drink 8 full glasses of water every day.

Weekly, I do 15 minutes of stretch exercises on Monday, Wednesday, and Friday, and Saturdays at 5:50 in the morning, just prior to my three-mile walk. In addition, I do situps and pushups which make me feel like I'm Arnold Schwarzenegger!

I swim a mile every week on Tuesdays at 6:00 A.M. and I play racquetball every Saturday, where I run Mike and Bill into the ground. I love the way I look and the incredible feeling of being in top shape.

Sample Creed #3: Health/Fitness

I am as regular as the rising sun in the exercise and care of my physical body. My healthy body is a gift from God and I show my love for Him in the way I care for my body. For this reason I retire each night by 10:00 P.M. and arise at 6:00 A.M. I am refreshed and invigorated as I greet the day while it is still young. I feel a great surge of power and confidence by this expression of self-control.

Every weekday morning at 7:15 I follow a regular routine that includes 30 minutes of exercising the large muscle groups of my body aerobically and rhythmically (running, walking, biking, or swimming) and challenging my body to become stronger and more fit. Monday, Wednesday, and Friday I exercise at 140 beats per minute for a minimum of 20 minutes (with an appropriate warm-up and cool-down). Lifting weights every Wednesday at 6:00 P.M. and Saturday at 10:00 A.M. provides my body with excellent body tone and muscle definition.

Eating the right foods is becoming a habit for me. I savor the natural flavor of foods. I particularly enjoy fresh vegetables and fruits and the whole grains. I love these high-fiber, low-fat, complex carbohydrates and find myself using no salt in my diet. Reading labels has become second nature to me and I treat items that are high in refined carbohydrates or fats as if they had a skull and crossbones on them. Taking three vitamins with each meal and three Omega-3 fatty acid capsules with dinner is also a habit that helps me feel terrific.

As I visualize myself with a 30-inch waist and moderate tan I know I can feel comfortable in any group, and my wife drools over how good-looking I have become.

My Relationship with My Family

Sample Creed #1: Family

Because my family is important to me, I find at least five minutes to talk to each member of the family every day. With my hands empty I make direct eye contact and my eyes and facial expression say "I love you." Each day I tell each member how much I love them. I look for the positive aspects of their lives and compliment them.

I seek to know what is happening in the lives of my family because I talk with them; and when we talk I really listen to what they are saying. I say kind and pleasant words because I am in control. Even when I am angry, I can show my displeasure while at the same time communicating my love and concern.

The center of my affection is my wife, Sue. Even though I love all members of the family, I let her know each day that she is the center of my love and that she is the source of happiness for me. I let her know that her smiles, cheerfulness, intelligence, and wit make life joyful. Every day for 15 minutes at bedtime, I share with her the occurrences of the day and I tell her of at least one of her positive qualities and at least one thing she has done that I appreciate.

Every Friday my sweetheart and I have a date. During the date I continually court Sue's affection and seek counsel and guidance from her as to how to be a better father, a better husband, and a better person. I listen to her answers, especially when she has criticism. I respect her so much that when she has suggestions for improving my life, I put them in my life creed and I begin working on the suggestions immediately. Because she is my love, I share my innermost desires, fears, and dreams with her.

Because I love and respect each member of my family, I want them to grow emotionally, intellectually, spiritually, and physically. I provide opportunities for individual growth regardless of the obstacles that come up. I strive to provide opportunities for each child to be challenged and to actually crystallize what he or she believes.

I reserve every Saturday for family activities and we have an activity night every Monday evening. The last Sunday of each month we have a family meeting to plan our Saturday activities and our vacations. We plan in detail for the next month and lay outlines for the entire year. Each month we update the master schedule. When an activity is scheduled, we follow through and complete that activity. These activities are so much fun that everyone can look forward to the planning meeting just for a chance to discuss them.

We have Family Council on Sunday evenings at 7:00. Even when I am not teaching the lesson I am prepared with stories, object lessons, or other material to help whoever is giving the lesson and to reinforce the things that Sue and I are teaching the family.

Sue and I take eight weekends each year (scheduled in our twelve-month calendar) away from our family and spend them together. We always go to some very romantic place and get to know each other again as we gain perspective on our lives, our marriage, and our family. The children enjoy the weekends when we are away too because we always employ such excellent babysitters.

Sample Creed #2: Family

Because I am so happy with myself, I'm happy with those around me, especially my family. I am easy to get along with—tolerant and pleasant. I realize that I cannot change my wife, so I work on improving myself. I treasure the time I spend with my family. I look forward to getting home and being with them. As I get closer to home I put my business cares aside and think about how much my wife and the kids need my strength and great attitude.

I have been blessed with the greatest family in the world.

I have a special day set aside every week for each of my children when I think about how much I love and appreciate them. I concentrate on the worth of each one as a child of God and on the talents and special gifts they have been blessed with. On their special day I spend a minimum of twenty minutes, one on one, seeking for ways I can serve them better. I always ask how I can be a better father and person, and I listen on their special day. Bill's day is Monday. I am grateful for his striving to do what's right and for his obedience. I look for ways to help him share his feelings more.

Brad is Tuesday. I appreciate his fun-loving nature and the way he makes us all laugh and feel good. I work hard to help him appreciate the value of schooling and the importance of his desire to get good grades.

Steve is Wednesday. He is a hard worker when he's able, and he has a tender heart underneath. By my example, I teach him the value of life without drugs and alcohol.

Thursday is Susie's day. She is so tender and concerned about others and has great sensitivity to their needs. I constantly strive to teach her to assert herself more and stand up for what she believes. I want each of the children to know that they are unique and that they have special gifts.

I love taking my beautiful wife on a date every Friday. I am absolutely committed to this special time with my precious companion and nothing comes before her. I ask her how I can be a better husband, father, and person, and I listen without defense. I put her suggestions in my Creed so I can start implementing them immediately.

I strive to lead my family in being creative in the activities we do together. My goal for our family is to see that we go camping once a month in the summer, hiking in the mountains twice a month, and skiing twice a month in the winter. I see to it that we swim once a week in the summer. We plan all of these activities the first Thursday of each month at 7:30 P.M. We go over the events of the coming month and schedule the coming year in advance.

Without fail I always support my children by being at their school activities and sporting events.

My wife always comes first, then the kids, in my priorities. Church and business come next.

Everyone knows by my actions how important my family is to me, including my family themselves.

I tell everyone in my family I love them every day. I hug them at least once a day and kiss them as I leave each morning. I give my wife an extra long hug and a big kiss every morning as we depart and every afternoon as we meet again. I show her by word and/or deed every day how glad I am that I married her.

My positive example and loving manner with my family creates an atmosphere of love and harmony in our home. My wife and children know they can come to me no matter how they feel and can count on me being a good listener and having lots of understanding. I always ask them how they are doing and I listen.

Sample Creed #3: Family

I am the patriarch of my family and I take this role most seriously. I love my family more than anything in this world. As I picture my sweetheart Mary, our pure and precious Susie, and our valiant son Jim, my heart wells with emotion and love. I recommit to keep all of my Creed's covenants and the Lord's commandments. I realize the predominant spirit in the home is a reflection of my spirit. For this reason I am patient and longsuffering with my sweetheart and children. My attention is focused first on them and their needs and how I can make life more rewarding and fun for them. They are always welcome in my office or on my lap; I greet them with a smile in my eyes to show how excited I am to have them with me. My extended family and friends and my own family are in awe of the consideration and Christlike kindness I show my immediate family.

I lead them every evening in family prayer. Forcing all other cares and concerns out of my mind, I plead with my Father in Heaven to protect and guide each member of our family. Our family bible study is actually so fun that if any members happen to miss it, they should feel a loss. Our family councils are planned at least one week in advance so the entire family can anticipate activities. Lessons are also important enough that we take turns as parents giving them and spend at least one hour in lesson preparation each week. Just being together as a family, no matter what we are doing, is an ideal situation I strive for. We hold our family council on Sundays from 6:00 P.M. on as sacred, allowing no other thing to interfere with this time together. My spirit of cheerfulness and optimism has a tremendous impact in overcoming any negative influence that may try to slip into our home to keep us from having and enjoying this time together.

I am also extremely sensitive to my bride's needs. I know that I am the greatest source of earthly love that my wife constantly receives and I strive to keep it constant. When I sense she is discouraged or frustrated, I demonstrate my endless love by dropping whatever is on my agenda and giving her my time. She is constantly surprised by the little gifts I give that show her I am thinking of just her each day. If I'm going to be later than I told her, I call and let her know what's happened and reaffirm my love for her! I place this call regardless of inconvenience. Whenever I return home, I first seek her out and share with her my appreciation to be her sweetheart. Every Friday night our date night is held sacred and no outside force is allowed to interfere. During these times I push out of my mind the cares of the day and concentrate on having fun with Mary. I also ask her every Friday during our date how I can be a better husband and father; then I actively listen to her answer and apply it to my life.

I also find it a joy to spend at least 30 minutes daily with one child in one-on-one time. I do this every Monday and Wednesday with Susie and every Tuesday and Thursday with Jim. During these precious moments we do whatever they want to do. They have total control of this agenda and I listen. This is an opportunity to show my unconditional love for them. I continually tell them that regardless of what happens in life I will always love and care for them. Over the years these weekly times together add up to hundreds of hours of quality time with my children. I'm so deeply grateful I am making this investment in my relationship with them.

Sample Creed #4: Family

Every day I look for ways to be a great dad and a terrific husband. I seek to create a feeling of peace, trust, harmony, happiness, and love in our home. It is indeed a heaven on earth! Through my efforts, I create the atmosphere in our home where my wife and children can feel that our home is a "safe haven"an oasis-from all worldly influence. This is due to the fantastic communication I am developing with each member of the family.

Every Friday night is "date night" with Diane. This time is for entertainment and relaxation, and, most importantly, for open communication about our relationship. I always express gratitude and love for Diane as my wife and best friend. I specifically point out the things I appreciate about her during the week. I continually let her know of my confidence in her as mother and teacher of our children. During date night I ask how I can be a better husband, father, and person— and I listen. My increasing ability to accept and immediately act upon her suggestions is one of my strongest traits. I keep Diane constantly aware of my business activities and our financial situation. I convey my innermost feelings to her so that she understands me completely and knows I need her.

My children also benefit from my excellent communication skills. Every week I spend a minimum of twenty minutes in an individual session with Karen, Mark, and Erin. Monday is Karen's day, Tuesday Mark and Wednesday Erin. In these session I ask each of them how I can be a better dad. Then I listen carefully with undivided interest to whatever they want to talk about, whether it's seeking fatherly counsel and advice or just "shooting the breeze." I use this time for positive communication. Discipline or reproving is saved for another time, and even then it is done in a manner of loving concern. On their day I focus on talking about their gifts and blessings and only address one area of concern I might have. Each Thursday, on a rotating basis, I take each of the kids on a "daddy-date-night." These dates are always scheduled in advance on our twelve-month calendar. My total focus is on them and how I can assist them in developing their gifts and easing their fears.

I let Karen know what a joy she is to be around with her subtle sense of humor. I tell her how blessed she is that God gave her creative a hand for art. Along with her physical beauty she has a very sensitive and caring nature; I express this to her often.

Mark is intelligent and bright-also very coordinated and skillful in athletics for his age. I tell him every day how proud I am to be his father, because of his willingness to always do what is right and honest.

Erin is extremely bubbly and fun-loving. She makes friends easily. I thank her often for coming to our home, for we need her constant reminding to have prayer and family time together.

I am blessed to have such heavenly spirits in my home. I express unconditional love to each child often—individually and collectively so they know their dad loves all of them. I show no favoritism. Through my words and actions, my children know of their worth and importance to their family and friends.

The consistency of our date nights and communication sessions draws us closer together as a family. I am the greatest source of earthly love that Diane and the children receive.

While at home I schedule my activities very carefully so I maximize the quality time I spend with the family. I enjoy playing with the kids and helping Diane with household duties in the evening. I read the newspaper only when it doesn't infringe on time which should be spent with members of my family or tasks that I am asked to do.

I take time every evening to discuss the day's events with Diane. This is done after the kids are in bed or when working together cleaning up the kitchen and dinner dishes.

Through my actions my wife and children know I love and care for them more than anything or anyone else in this world and they know I need them as much as they need me. I look for ways to let them serve me. Every family member is reminded by me of his importance to the whole family which helps to maintain their own self-worth and individualism.

Sample Creed #5: Family

My wife is the most important person in the world to me. She is the center of my life and I cherish her. I love her and I look for ways to make her happy. I compliment my sweetheart and I look for, notice, and express appreciation for the things she does for the kids and me.

I accept her as she is and do all I can to create an atmosphere that allows her to grow and bloom into the choice woman she wants to be. I include her in my life, both business and personal. I talk with her and seek her advice. I trust her, feel close to her, and am strengthened by her.

I search for ways to show her affection. I let her know my feelings. I express myself to her. When dealing with her and the children I make it a top priority to remain in control of my voice and my temper. My presence in the home creates an atmosphere of unity, peace, and serenity.

I am sensitive to her feelings. I enjoy giving her the things she desires. She is special and important to me, and I express this to her each day. I help her with the house and look for ways to lighten her load. I compliment her on her appearance and I keep myself in good shape to inspire her to get in and/or stay in good shape.

I am her friend and confidant—someone she can lean on and trust and depend on for support. I strive to deserve the title, "her best friend." Every week on Friday night my sweetheart and I have our date night. I bring home food or the kids take care of dinner themselves. We go out by ourselves and I concentrate on being a great communicator with her. I ask her how I can be a better father, husband, and person and I listen. Nothing comes before my sweetheart on our date night.

My children are individuals with ideas and feelings. I seek for their counsel and advice where appropriate. I know that asking my children for input adds a very special dimension to our relationship and helps us to be much closer, sharing concern for each other and being more aware of each other's needs and feelings. They are also much more receptive to advice when I do this.

Sample Creed #6: Family

(Grandfather) I am the patriarch of my family and I take this important role very seriously. The Lord has blessed me with the greatest wife in the world and five beautiful children. My wife is my best friend and confidant. I make sure we have the opportunity every night to talk about the day's activities and tomorrow's events. I share my successes and problems in business with her. She is so helpful and understanding and assists me through any personal or business problems that I am concerned about. I enjoy being with her and there is usually nothing I ask her to do that she's not willing to do. In turn, I respond to her wishes and cherish her. I focus on being unselfish with her and when I talk to her it is in a loving tone of voice, which creates a wonderful atmosphere for her to enjoy.

I laugh and cry with her and express each day how much I love her and how important she is to me. I love to give her "warm fuzzies" and surprise her regularly with small gifts of appreciation.

At least once every year I write a letter of appreciation to her and tell her how much joy she brings to me. She is Number One on my list of priorities. I talk to her during the day and let her know she's the greatest. I love to hold hands and walk arm in arm wherever we go. Every Thursday night we go out to dinner and talk about "how I am doing." I take her suggestions and implement them into my life. I use my LifeCreed to help me remember to do this. I would rather play golf, tennis, and ride horses with her than anyone. She is so positive that it makes me the same way. I dwell on her many positive traits and ignore the negatives. If there is anything that upsets me, I diplomatically bring it to her attention in a loving way. We spend a lot of time together and it is all quality.

I'm very proud of my children, and even though they are married, I still contact them weekly—either personally or by phone—to inquire after their well-being and to express my love. I hug and kiss them each time I see them, and I seek to end every conversation by letting them know how much I love and respect them. Quarterly on a Tuesday I take each one to lunch and ask "How am I doing?" "Can I be of help?" or "How can I serve you or your family better?" I treat their spouses the same way and make them feel like sons and daughters. Whenever I speak of someone in front of other children, it is positive. If I can't say something good about every child, I don't say anything. I look for each child's strengths and help that child develop them.

I make it a top priority to keep our traditional Memorial Day, July 4, and Labor Day family gatherings at the cabin full of love and unity, which I always teach by example. Whether I'm with my children or away from them I conduct myself in a way that they can be proud of my actions or words. Every December I have an annual interview with each one of my children to see how I'm doing as a dad and how I can help them if necessary. They always know they can call on me for anything and I will help them through thick and thin. I create the atmosphere where my grandchildren, whether they are here or out of state, would rather be with me than anyone. I am fun-loving with them and let them know how special they are. I attend my local grand-children's sports activities, school functions, and other activities as I can. I support them in all they do. Both children and grandchildren know how interested I am in them by the attention I give them.

All my children know how much I love their mom and know of our special relationship. We are an excellent example to them.

My Relationship with Others: Social

Sample Creed #1: Social

I love people and I am thankful for my opportunities to interact with those around me. I enjoy talking with others and being able to help them by giving wise counsel when they come to me for help. I look for the good qualities in others and make a special point of giving honest compliments and praise. I am tolerant of values and back-grounds which are different from my own. I see each person as a son or daughter of God and allow that person his or her weaknesses.

I am a fantastic conversationalist. I keep myself well informed and am able to discuss current events and issues intelligently. I do this by reading the newspaper and my magazine subscriptions every day during my lunch hour. People are amazed at how conversant and knowledge-able I am. My favorite practice is to "interview" whomever I am talking to. I am fascinated by people's stories. I am a warm and loving person. I create an atmosphere of comfort and safety when others are confiding in me. I have a great sense of humor and am able to use that talent to put others at ease and relieve tension when appropriate.

I have a talent for putting my thoughts into words. When I am having a conversation with someone, I am assertive and able to say what I am thinking and feeling in a concise and interesting way, being tactful and diplomatic. I listen empathetically and actively while the other person is talking, concentrating on what he or she is saying and the feelings behind the words.

I feel comfortable entertaining friends and colleagues in my home or attending social functions. I am a gracious ambassador on behalf of my husband and always speak well of him to others. In the community I am active in voicing my opinions and encourage others to do so. I attend PTA meetings and parent/teacher conferences because I believe it is important for me to know what my children are being taught and what sort of environment they are being taught in. I research political issues and learn the views of candidates, actively supporting those with whom I agree and opposing those candidates or issues I am against.

Sample Creed #2: Social

I have the most fantastic and enjoyable life imaginable. I love every minute of it because I am proud of what and who I am. Even though I am very satisfied with my life, I am doing more so that it is getting even better.

I care about everyone I meet and so I'm anxious to make new acquaintances. I make it easy for people to like me because they can tell I care; I listen to what they say by looking them in the eye and giving them my undivided attention. I observe a good point about each person I meet and mention it when appropriate. I use it to remember that person. I love being where people are and getting to know them.

I express my opinions but am very careful to understand the opinions and feelings of others. I strive to keep my opinions based on sound facts and change them only when better information shows my errors.

I like laughter and have good times but never at the expense of others. I am the first to laugh at my own mistakes but work hard to help others not feel self-conscious or ill at ease when they make mistakes.

I am a good and loyal friend. I work to keep informed of my friends' successes and trials. I am there when I'm needed but quickly disappear when I am in the way.

I work hard to help all people know how fragile and delicate our environment is. I work to stimulate people's minds so that they realize their lives are greatly improved by working to clean the air, purify the water, and avoid unnecessary waste.

I show people by example that an individual can make a significant contribution toward improving life by reducing consumption and preserving resources. I conserve resources by developing energy-saving programs for my home, business, and community.

Sample Creed #3: Social

I love to share my thoughts and feelings when I am in a group of people. I look for ways to share ideas and experiences that uplift others around me.

I am blessed with great insight and wisdom in the area of human relations. People feel at ease in my presence and are in awe of my many special talents and abilities.

I am a fantastic listener. I am increasingly more effective in my ability to zero in on what people are thinking and feeling. I always listen for five minutes for what someone is feeling before I speak. This great skill allows me to become intimately involved in people's lives in a very short time. People who trust me with their innermost feelings can have complete confidence that I will not violate that trust.

I am a very active listener, especially with my wife and my wonderful children. They are in awe of how well I listen to them without defensive rebuff.

People love being around me, not only because I am very outgoing, but because they can talk to me on their own level knowing that I listen attentively and give them honest feedback. They realize that I am a man of high moral conduct and that I am totally honest in my dealings.

I feel good about myself. Each day I am in greater control of my life and know that my conduct is becoming more and more the epitome of what my God expects of me.

Sample Creed #4: Social

I endeavor to go out of my way to welcome others into my presence by greeting them warmly with a kind word. I listen to them carefully, looking them in the eye, my hands empty. I realize the value of a friendly face and an outstretched arm in making others feel they are of value and in a secure place.

I provide opportunities for my children to practice good manners and acceptable social graces so that they can develop the skills they need to be welcomed by others on social occasions. I invite guests into our home on a weekly basis in order to provide these teaching experiences, and our visitors enjoy a hospitable and pleasant experience as well.

I remember my Southern heritage and am sensitive to the feelings and customs of those I am around. I support their needs and desires to accomplish their goals and to have pride in their heritage. I help my children understand this by giving them opportunities to mingle with those who are not in their peer group.

My Relationship with Job and Money

Sample Creed #1: Career/Financial

I am a true professional in the life insurance business: I look sharp and I am highly organized.

I always begin my workday knowing exactly where I am headed. I have a well-developed system that maximizes the use of my time and energies. A color-coded weekly chart is the key to this system. I keep it before me all during my workday, and it shows me at all times what my ideal workweek consists of. I constantly strive to fill my week with the activities that are recorded on the chart. By keeping a written record of my activities I am always aware of where I am in relation to where I should be. This makes me stretch and grow each week as I strive to have my actual week match up with my ideal week. I have eight priorities I am committed to accomplish each day. As I accomplish each priority I color code it with green, indicating that it has been done. I know that this system gives me a slight edge and magnifies my results tenfold.

I always set up a minimum of 15 interviews per week. Of these at least five are new interviews. This assures me I'll end up with consistent results each week.

One of my greatest assets is my enthusiasm and self-discipline. I am in my office by 7:45 A.M. and I leave at 6:00 P.M. I always remember to record my activity and pinpoint the areas where I am improving my effectiveness. I always have my prospects and clients meet me in my office during the daytime. This gives me the feeling of being a true professional.

When I set a goal I know I can achieve it because I clearly define it and know the amount and type of activity that is required to achieve it.

Over the next twelve-month period I am doing the things that lead to $72,000 in commissions. This breaks down to $1,500 per week for 48 working weeks.

On October 1 of this year I am debt free and have $10,000 in the bank. We move into our new home on October 2. This new home is in the Cedar Breaks area, which allows my children to remain in the school they are accustomed to.

My wife is shouting for joy because she no longer works outside the home as she finishes her degree.

On July 7 of this year I have a new Cadillac Coupe de Ville. It is white with a beautiful red interior, cruise control, air-conditioning, and power windows and seats. This beautiful machine makes me feel very secure and powerful.

I really love this business and love what it does for my family. I know that there is no other business in the world that gives more personal freedom and financial independence. I am 100% committed to excellence in my career and am grateful that my God has blessed me so abundantly.

Sample Creed #2: Career/Financial

Financially I have the ideal life. In two years I earn $160,000 per year which allows me to take care of all the temporal needs of my family. I meet all of my financial obligations with ease. I have extraordinary money-handling capabilities and I am mastering the budgeting for both my personal and family financial affairs.

I automatically set aside 40% of my earnings in a separate account earmarked for all taxes and church obligations. I give Cheryl $2,000 each month for basic monthly expenditures on home and family needs. In addition, she receives $500 each month which is allocated for gifts, kids' clothing, Christmas fund, and her personal savings. This leaves me with $65,000 to fund the following areas:

Children's Trusts: I have set up a trust fund for each of my kids. Every year I place $5,000 into separate trust accounts for Susan, Tom, and Monica. These funds are only used for education and emergencies, plus a future resource to help springboard them in starting up a business or to begin financial plans for their own kids' education, etc.

Personal Planning for Cheryl and Myself: I use $20,000 each year for funding our own savings, insurance, retirement, and estate plans. This includes fees associated with creating and maintaining sound and proper estate-planning documents (will, trust, agreements, etc).

The "Fun Fund:" This is my reward for all the blood, sweat, and tears used in generating this income and religiously sticking to my financial plan. The remaining $30,000 in the annual budget is discretionary dollars used for special business opportunities or charitable projects. I have a keen sense for recognizing honest and profitable business ideas. I am full of charity toward all men, women, and children and give willingly to charities which serve to benefit the youth-particularly the abused and homeless. I love to give!

I use the "Fun Fund" to purchase a new car every three years. I also invest in rare sports cars and collect them. Every year I plan two major vacations which are financed from this fund. I plan one with the entire family. The other is a vacation and annual planning retreat with Cheryl only. These trips are planned in advance and scheduled on the twelve-month calendar. In addition, I take Cheryl on a spur-of-the-moment getaway for two or three days. During the next eight years, Cheryl and I have visited Hawaii, Western Europe, Israel, Australia, New Zealand, and the Orient.

In eight years on January 1, I have $100,000 in liquid and semi-liquid resources for any emergency or opportunity which may come along. This is formed from the "Fun Fund," and if it is ever dipped into it is my main priority to build it back up as quickly as possible, even if it requires using all of the "Fun Fund" for the year, or more.

Above all, I use the utmost prudence and sensibility when spending money. I always exercise total honesty and integrity when investing.

Some Additional Sample LifeCreed Statements

Over the years my female clients have offered sample creed statements regarding improving their relationship with their husbands.

Note to Men: As you review the following statements, convert them into the masculine and use them in your own LifeCreed.

- I feel extremely honored to be a wife. Because I am supportive, understanding, and caring, my husband feels it an honor and a blessing to be married to me.

- I am aware that making love is a twenty-four-hour-a-day process for me. It means I take time for him, and I develop an attitude and an environment which brings out the goodness in each of us through my loving, caring attention to him.

- The highlight of my day is the time we spend together. No matter what I'm doing, it's more fun with John. We joke and laugh; we find a zillion ways to do little things for each other.

- I keep a list of all his favorite things and another list of all the things I admire in him, so I'm always armed with warm fuzzies. I have an unlimited supply of hugs and kisses to keep his reservoir filled. Not a day passes without my sharing my intense love for him.

- I am competent, self-assured, well-groomed, easy to be with, and approving of him. I make him feel competent, attractive, masculine, romantic, young, intelligent, appreciated, wanted, needed, cherished, and loved.

- I'm adept at resolving differences that may stand between our oneness.

- When it comes to intimacy, I am relaxed, receptive, and warm. I'm understanding of any concerns, positive, and self confident. I'm feminine yet aggressive on occasion.

- He loves my back rubs, foot rubs, or body rubs, which help relax both of us and sends a message to him that his pleasure is worth my time.

- I make it my business to be aware of his needs and desires. I find out what he likes and how he likes it, and I give love to him just that way, sharing with him my undiluted, undivided attention.

- I also communicate to him my needs and preferences, my pleasure, and my enjoyment of being close to him.

- Romance is alive in me and I bring it to life in him!

- I am the bride he always dreamed of, the sweetheart he continues dreaming of, the lover he'll never tire of.

More Sample LifeCreed Statements

Here are some wonderful sample LifeCreed statements submitted by women for improving peace and love in the home and harmony in life.

(Again, men, convert these to the masculine and use them in your LifeCreed.)

- When my priorities are challenged, my husband is first, then my children.

- I treat my husband and children with courtesy and respect. I think the best of them, saying only good about them to others.

- I treat my husband and children with unconditional love. When my children do something good I feel like telling everyone. They know how proud I am and that I'm always for them.

- I want the best for my fine husband and my beautiful children. I make the atmosphere in our home a comfortable place for my family to learn, grow, and retreat to.

- When people walk into my home they immediately feel a sense of excitement, a zest for life, as if the sun were going to burst right into their arms.

- Everyday I seek to think and do the things that make me the happiest, brightest girl in the world.

- Sunshine is my trademark. Next to my smile, even the sun takes a back seat!

- I am constantly smiling, always laughing, always ready for a good time. I have a spring in my step that makes others think I'm going to take off and fly.

- I am enthusiastic. I am excited about life and spontaneous in my actions.

- I'm positive and excited about new ideas and suggestions.

- Positive Mental Attitude is my middle name.

- I am easy to please. Even the smallest pleasures make my day. I am easy to be with, fun-loving, easy-going, and flexible.

- I warmly welcome visitors and make them feel glad they came. When my schedule can't accommodate lengthy visits, I always make them want to return.

- When those burdened with sorrow knock on my door, they leave with lifted hearts and brighter spirits, having greater faith in tomorrow.

- I radiate love, virtue, goodness, and nobility.

- I am so happy when the children awake each morning. I eagerly convey to them my love and delight in being their mother.

247

- I am especially delighted in being able to help members of my family.

- I am a peacemaker. I offer solutions, not problems.

- I am teachable. I enjoy learning from others and make changes when a change is for the best.

- I think for five minutes before talking about an emotionally upsetting subject.

- I strive to have childlike qualities-quick to love, quick to forgive, and quick to forget.

- I show frequent signs of affection daily to my family and express my love and gratitude for them many times each day.

- I honestly listen to my husband and children and am sensitive to their need for a listening ear.

- I maintain a 9-1 ratio of positive-negative comments with my children. I genuinely praise every effort they make and give special praise whenever they make good choices. I ensure that good choices get more attention than wrong choices.

- Each disciplinary session is a positive learning experience. I discipline with love and gentleness.

- I feel exhilarated when my home is clean. Keeping it in order is so second nature to me I hardly realize I'm doing it.

- I take time to help my children learn how to care for our home. We have a great time working together.

- I teach my children to love work and take pride in doing their best.

- I include good music in every area of my family's life. I teach my children to enjoy uplifting, beautiful music.

- I take twenty minutes each weekday just to play with and talk to my children—Monday and Friday at 9:00 A.M. with Carson; Tuesday and Thursday with Tiffany; and Wednesday and Saturday at noon with Amber.

- I include our parents in our lives by making them a vital part of our children's lives. I express frequently my love and appreciation for all they do. We spend at least two evenings a month visiting or writing them.

- I spend a fun evening with my husband each Friday night, when we just relax, enjoy each other, and have a great time.

- I say I'm sorry whenever unkind feelings arise, regardless of whose fault it is. I readily admit when I'm wrong.

- I have a family planning session with Steve every second Sunday at 6:30 P.M.

- I frequently ask how I can be a better wife and mother.

- I am constantly striving to be better.

- When I make a mistake I realize tomorrow's a new day and that I'm still a great person. I am strong and wise enough to forgive myself and refocus on the things that matter.

- I have a special affinity for and talent with the youth. I make it a point to search them out when they're around. I always try to build their confidence and self-esteem.

- I am a leader among women. Many look to me as a role model for strength and courage.

249

- People love to be around me because I only say positive and uplifting things about others.

- I have a unique ability to put my thoughts and feelings into appropriate words and always have something meaningful to talk about.

- I practice and teach my children to have good manners. I provide opportunities for them to learn social skills by inviting guests to our home and allowing the children to participate in formal visiting.

- Family priorities take precedence over time conflicts. I have the courage to graciously bow out of social responsibilities when they conflict by saying, "I'd love to but I have a prior commitment."

- I retire at 10:30 P.M. and arise at 6:00 A.M. sharp to greet each beautiful new day!

- I cannot blame my genes, but I am the one who must wear my jeans. Therefore, I keep my body strong, gorgeous and desirable. I exercise five days a week—Monday to Friday from 6:45–7:30 A.M. I bike or jog, keeping my exercise heart rate at 134 BPM for thirty minutes on Monday, Wednesday, and Friday. I have Pritikin-type eating habits that keep me in the best of health. All I ever want of treats or desserts is a taste.

- I think, act, feel and look young. People who don't know me think, "What a cool lady."

- I do what is necessary to maintain the youthful, vigorous body of a twenty-year old. I am totally committed to my exercise program and proper nutrition.

- I am able to function at peak performance and physically do anything I want to.

- My mind functions with a keenness and clarity not possible without physical exercise and good nutrition. I feel great about myself.

- When Steve sees my lean, tan, 120-pound body with my perfect dimensions and beautiful blond hair, it mesmerizes him.

- I am well-read and love to delve into the intellectual reservoirs of this life. I choose from the best reading materials.

- I've been blessed with many talents and don't hide them. I share them with others for their benefit and mine.

- I support and encourage my husband in his work. By showing interest in his work and spending time discussing business, I let him know that I also place importance on how he spends much of his time. When he comes home late from work or needs to spend home-time doing business, I always assume that he is doing what he feels is best for our family.

- I have the courage and skills to tactfully discuss priorities if they seem to get out of balance.

- I maintain good professional habits by (1) improving public relations skills; (2) always keeping myself well-groomed and attractive; (3) occasionally taking classes relating to my professional interests; (4) frequently using my secretarial skills for others and for my personal needs; and (5) keeping my eyes open for other effective ways of earning money.

- One of my current responsibilities is to help secure our financial future. I do that by thinking not what I can buy, but what I can

251

do without and how I can save. I am frugal and provident in the purchasing of food, clothing, gifts, and the like.

- I admire so much the generosity of my husband and know we'll both find much happiness as we create financial stability for our family, using what we gain to bless the lives of others.

COMPLETE LifeCreed Samples

The following completed LifeCreeds reflect each individual's perception of his or her ideal self and ideal life. Many of these ideals were not yet realized when the Creeds were written.

As you study them, look for ideas you may have missed in your own LifeCreed. Some of the areas emphasized may not reflect your hopes, dreams, and aspirations, while others may. These are private and important for these individuals, so please respect them. (Names have been changed to ensure anonymity.)

Putting it All Together for Men

Young Father

I love my life. I have outstanding potential and I am accomplishing great things.

I have the most wonderful family and I love them very much. Debbie is terrific. I am so blessed to have her for my companion. I constantly work at keeping my relationship with her fantastic. She knows how much I love her because I always consider her feelings and place her first in my life. I demonstrate my affection and respect for her by treating her like a true gentleman does, opening doors for her and getting up when she enters a room of guests. I constantly look for ways to serve her and make her happy. I ask her how I can best help her at home and promptly follow through with her requests.

I love Debbie very much. She is my best friend and I enjoy being with her. I know I can't change my wife, so I work on improving myself. I know the love and respect I show to her in the presence of our children increases the love and harmony in our home. I create an atmosphere of peace, trust, happiness, harmony, and love in our home. In times of tension and stress in our home I am calm and control my voice and temper. My wife and children are in awe of how cool I am.

Debbie comes first in my life, then my children, then church and business. The center of my affection is Debbie. Even though I love all the children, I let Debbie know every day that she is the center of my love and that she is the source of my greatest happiness. I let her know how much her thoughtfulness, kindness and caring for me, the kids, and others means to me. Every evening at bedtime I look forward to talking to her for 15 minutes, finding out about the occurrences in her day and asking questions that will help to pull out the feelings she wants to share.

I reserve every Friday night for Debbie. It is our date night. During the date I give her affection and seek counsel and guidance from her in how to be a better father, husband, and person. I put her suggestions in my Creed and immediately start working on implementing them. I look for opportunities to court her each day of the week. I show her how much I love her through my actions and by telling her I love her each day. I find a "warm fuzzy" each day to do for her. I kiss her each night and tell her I love her.

Because she is my love, I share my innermost desires, fears, and. dreams with her.

Debbie and I discipline the children together in a joint effort. We discuss problems each evening and jointly decide on the solutions.

I am a great dad. Through my efforts I create an atmosphere in our home where my wife and children can feel that our home is "heaven on earth," a safe place to return from all worldly influence. This is created by the love I demonstrate toward Debbie.

Everyone, including my family members, knows by my actions how important my family is to me. I tell everyone in my family I love them every day. I know what is happening in the lives of my family members because I communicate with them and really listen to what they are saying. I look them in the eye and give them my total attention.

As I drive home after work each day I concentrate on unwinding and releasing the daily stress before the garage door opens. After I enter the garage I sit in the car for 3 minutes and spend quiet time alone before I enter the house. Then when I enter our home, I greet my wife and children with joy; I am happy to be with them.

Debbie and I have a planning session once each week on Sunday at 9:00 P.M. when we plan our upcoming activities. We discuss our goals and dreams, and we spend time talking about and planning our future.

Because my family is important, I always look for the positive aspects in their lives and compliment them. I love my kids and I always relate to them in a kind and loving manner. I influence them "only by persuasion, by longsuffering, by gentleness and meekness, and by love unfeigned. By kindness and pure knowledge ... without hypocrisy and without guile." Each week I have a special day set aside for my sons and I focus on each one on his day. I show my love by concentrating on helping him to reach his potential.

Monday is for Brett. He has such a unique spirit. I always remember the inspiration I received the day he was born. I encourage his creativity, compliment his kindness, and especially set a good spiritual example for him.

Tuesday is for Billy. I love the way his face lights up when he smiles. I encourage him in his athletics and spend time playing with him. I pay particular attention to his need for positive recognition and always look for ways to compliment him.

Wednesday is for Bobby. I love him for the joy he brings into my life. I take time to be affectionate with him and to enjoy his tender years.

The spiritual progress and development of my family are very important. I always lead out so we have family council every Sunday at 7:00 P.M. We pray and sing together, then we have a spiritual lesson which I prepare. I always ask my family how I can improve and I listen to what they say.

I feel comfortable entertaining friends and colleagues in my home or attending social functions. I am a great conversationalist. People love to talk to me. I keep myself well informed on current issues and am able to discuss them intelligently. I am approachable and have a great sense of humor. I use my talents to entertain and put others at ease.

When I am having a conversation with someone, I am assertive and say what I think in a clear, concise, and interesting way. I am an active listener, concentrating on what others say and the feelings behind their words.

I have a fantastic memory, especially for people's names. When meeting someone new I always use his or her name three times in the first conversation. I create a name association and hook which enables me to instantly recall the name the next time we meet. I have great ability to recall information about finance, current events, and other items of interest. I love to learn and am hungry for information. Because of my excellent memory friends and associates come to me for the wealth of information I am able to recall.

Every day I am in more control of my thoughts and actions because I always seek to act as if the Lord were here with me. Whenever inappropriate thoughts enter my mind I replace them by singing Come Unto Jesus. The most important part of my day is the time I spend with my Lord. I search the scriptures every evening before going to bed and spend 10 minutes in mighty prayer. I pray earnestly each morning and again at noon and always carry a prayer in my heart.

I gather my family together for family prayer before we leave the house each day and upon retiring each night. I receive inspiration in my activities because I counsel with the Lord about the things I do and I listen for his direction.

I confide in those I serve and seek their advice as to how I can serve them better. I listen without defense and make specific commitments for improvement. I love the opportunities I have to serve others.

My office is located in Charleston Square and is tastefully appointed in the traditional decor of rich walnuts with accenting furnishings. My associates and clients are impressed with its subtle elegance. It exhibits an air of sophistication and success, yet is warm and inviting. People feel at ease and are comfortable when visiting.

The key to my success is commitment: first, to the success of my clients; second, to my goals; and third, to effective planning. I always begin my week with eight planning and four introduction appointments scheduled, because I follow my "Ideal Week" plan and have it in front of me continually. I know that the law of averages works in my favor, and as a result, I earn $3,000 weekly, $156,000 annually by June four years from now.

In two years on January 1, I have $25,000 in the bank. On July 1 in three years, we are completely out of debt. On January 1 four years from now, we purchase with cash our wooded building lot. By January 1 in five years, I have saved $50,000 and we begin construction on our new home. On August 1 in five years, we move in. Debbie has designed it beautifully. I particularly enjoy sitting on the back deck looking out into the yard and listening to the river passing by. I can feel the cool breeze rustling through the trees. From my bedroom window I love to listen to the song of birds in the distance.

I save $750 per month, putting $500 into permanent life insurance and the balance into investments. On July 1 in three years we have no debts outside of our home mortgage, which is paid off in 10 years. We use credit cards as a convenience and pay all our bills on or before their due dates.

I am proud of my body. I work very hard to build it into perfect proportions. Each day as I exercise, I clearly visualize my ideal body: my chest- measures 44 inches, my waist 32, my biceps 16, my thighs 23, and my calves 16. I weigh 195 lbs and my body fat is less than 10%. I measure myself on the first Monday of each month. At 6:00 A.M. on Monday, Tuesday, Thursday, and Friday I exercise for 60 minutes. I get my heartbeat up to its training rate of 140 and maintain it for 20 minutes. I follow a healthy diet consisting of fruits, vegetables, and quality proteins. This gives me tremendous energy and stamina and I feel great!

I listen to my Creed in the morning while driving to work and again while driving home. I carry a copy with me in my day planner and read it when I am waiting for appointments. This continually reminds me of who I am and keeps in focus my blessings, my talents, and my goals. My success continues to increase and I thank God for it.

Middle-Aged Father with Younger Children

I really have a great life. I am a good person to know. I am respected by the people who really know me because of my reputation for being a professional. People trust me because I care about them, and I help them get the things they want. I am respected by my peers as someone who is successful and willing to serve in professional organizations.

I am a successful manager. My office is tastefully decorated in mauve and grey, and some of my original photographs are expertly displayed. When people enter the office they notice the new carpet and wallpaper, the floral arrangements, and the new furniture. Many people comment on how professional the office looks. I am particular about the standards of cleanliness in my office and the image that is reflected as people enter.

I create an atmosphere that helps the people who work in this office feel that they are part of a professional team. I always wear professional-looking suits in dark, tasteful colors, solid-colored newly pressed shirts, and clean, sharp ties. I carry myself with authority and my manner is calm, befitting my position. I inspire confidence in my ability by the way I speak slowly and confidently. I look people straight in the eye and I listen carefully to what they say. I am relaxed in my manner and careful in my speech.

I have the uncanny ability to find and attract quality people who become self-motivated achievers because I strive to be aware of each employee. Each week I hold a personal performance review with each employee to let them know of my support for them and to help them identify and achieve their goals.

I have a nice home that is comfortable to be in and well-suited for having good times with friends. I enjoy having people over for swimming parties; they enjoy the pool area and the play yard, which I keep neatly trimmed and landscaped. The house is freshly painted and in good repair.

In the family room my friends and family enjoy the dynamic sound that comes from the JVC stereo system; we enjoy good movies on the Mitsubishi big-screen video monitor. It feels good to come home each day. My friends and associates always enjoy coming to my house because they feel comfortable there.

I am proud that I am able to give Nancy $3,000 each month for household expenses and that I have $1,000 each month to use as I please. I am proud of our home and our swimming pool and that we live in such a nice area.

I am married to a beautiful, dynamic woman. I am proud of Nancy and I encourage her to reach her best potential by developing her talents and abilities.

Nancy is action oriented; she has a good sense of her goals and what she wants to accomplish in her life, and she is working steadily toward them. She is overcoming her former feelings of low self-image by being fiercely competitive. She is respected by her peers and is gaining recognition in the community for her accomplishments.

259

Each day as I drive home from work, I think of something that I can say to compliment her. I get excited thinking how my kind words will make her feel, and I can't wait to get home to give her a loving hug, a tender kiss, and tell her that I love her.

I tell Nancy of my love for her each day. We are partners together in running the household and in raising the children. I reserve each Friday to spend with Nancy. This is our date night and we always do something by ourselves to bring us closer together. During these times I seek feedback on how I am doing as a husband and father.

I am always a gentleman, constantly courting her with thoughtful etiquette and good manners. Even when I am provoked I speak in low tones. I am fiercely loyal to her, both in her presence and when I am away from her. In public and in private I only say those things which build her esteem. I flirt with her and her alone. My behavior provokes no jealousy. I bring variety and tenderness into our sexual relations and feel my greatest satisfaction when Nancy is fulfilled.

I create an atmosphere where Nancy can be proud of my accomplishments and eager to share them with other people. I conduct myself around my family in a way that Nancy is inspired to tell my children how proud she is of me, encouraging them to be like me. I am calm and self-assured at home.

As I drive toward my home, I also begin to think of my children and how I can reinforce their individual strengths. I have a special day set aside every week for each of my children where I always spend 20 minutes, one on one, listening and sharing with them, asking how I can be a better father and person.

Monday is for Susan. I am proud that she is playing on the basketball team and that she is doing well in her classes. I enjoy being around her-she is my friend. My concern is that she develops a sense of urgency about her life, and that she will challenge herself to reach a greater potential, never satisfied with average performance.

Tuesday is for Shana. She is much like her mother and I am excited to think of the potential for achievement she has. I am proud of the growth I have seen in her these past two years. She is a compassionate person and is kind to people who may not have many friends. My concern is that she will be strong enough to lift others, but will not lower her own standards, even though her friends may exhibit lower standards of behavior. I am also concerned that she will be able to control her emotions as she begins to explore the world of boys.

Wednesday is for Robert. He is tender, sensitive, and good-looking. He is popular with his friends, yet is learning to be a leader in doing what he knows is right. I am proud of his accomplishments in the Boy Scouts, and I am committed to being with him for most of his activities. I am concerned that he will gain a strong character and sense of right behavior so that he will not be swayed when his friends tempt him to do something that is popular, yet wrong. I am also concerned about his health since he does not want to eat vegetables.

Thursday is for Tom, my athlete. He is feisty, physical, and very creative. He is emotional and enjoys all the physical attention I give him. I encourage his creative talents and help him with his soccer games. My concern for him is that I give him the affection and attention he needs to build a strong self-image. I also encourage him to keep his creative talent active and channel it into productive areas as he progresses in school.

Friday is for George, my most interesting challenge. He is very sensitive and needs lots of affection and attention. Of all the children he has the greatest need for individual attention. My commitment is to continually have the patience and wisdom to give him the individual attention he needs so that he may improve his reading and social skills. It appears that he will not be good at athletics and will likely be attracted to dramatic arts or music. I am excited to think of the great potential he has as he grows up.

Saturday is for Liz, my pride and joy. I am constantly pleased with the cute things she says and does. It is fun to watch her grow up; and its great to have a little girl around the house. My concern is to teach her good social skills and to be a responsible member of the family. I try to avoid giving her everything she wants, which could spoil her.

I write a letter to each member of my family every six months and share my feelings with them. Susan in January and July; Sharon in February and August; Robert in March and September; Tom in April and October; George in May and November; Liz in June and December. I write to Nancy at least every January and July.

I create an atmosphere where my children can develop self-confidence and discover their talents. I do this by being supportive and by showing my love for them constantly so that they can recognize the power within them to become anything they want to become.

I help my children learn common sense by using it in my own actions; wisdom by allowing them to make mistakes; and high moral values by being honest in my own dealings.

I pray for guidance in knowing how to better serve them.

I have a monthly planning session every first Sunday at 4:00 P.M. with my family. I conduct these meetings and we discuss the things we want to accomplish in the coming month and in the coming year. I record these things on a 12-month planning calendar that is kept in the office at home where everyone can look at it.

Quarterly we create a new tradition for our family, which I identify, and record in our family history book.

With my family I plan for the acquisition of everything we decide we want. This includes the vacations we will take, and the time we spend together, and it is written down in our yearly planning calendar.

I set an example of spirituality in my family by reading the bible and other inspirational books each day for 15 minutes before going to bed, always striving to know what Heavenly Father would have me do. I discuss my reading with my family when the opportunity presents itself.

I always get up before 6:30 A.M. and go through my exercise routine. I think of my flat stomach and my narrow waist as I do four sets of pushups, three sets of sit-ups, then ride the exercycle or jog in place. I get my heart rate up to 140 BPM for at least 20 minutes each day and I check it regularly. This keeps my heart strong and my waist trim. Because of my highly-conditioned, energetic body, Nancy can't resist coaxing me to quit working and to come to bed with her at night.

I go biking twice each week and climb each of the major peaks around the valley every year. I know that doing this maintains my weight at 160 pounds and my waist at 33 inches. People often comment on how good I look because I keep my abdomen flat and always have a smile. I always have energy to play with my children. My body feels better than it ever has and I am glad to be alive!

In my relationships I zero in on what others feel, think, and want—if I am confused I always check it out. I go beyond the superficial surface. I am an interpersonal explorer. I realize that anger is a defensive emotion and covers up either hurt or fear, so I am patient with angry people and try to discover what it is that is truly bothering them. I don't blame; I problem solve. I listen to understand and talk to be understood using feelings, thoughts, and wants. I then seek to identify the problem, brainstorm alternatives, and seek solutions and alternatives for a win/win solution. I allow others their freedom. I forgive others and myself. I allow us to be human and have our weaknesses and mistakes in life. I am increasingly patient and tolerant. I believe that I and others like me are trying to do our best and need support, love, understanding, recognition, praise, and forgiveness. I am a skilled communicator and teach others by my own example how to be intimate and loving. I consistently do a role-check with significant others, i.e., "How can I be a better boss, father, son, business man, psychologist, etc.?" I in turn am very disclosive. I allow myself to be interpersonally vulnerable.

I address people's needs: I strive to provide a safe, secure environment where people feel valued and respected and where they can grow and have variety. I ask what a person's vision and dreams are, what they want and need, and why they want it. Then I ask how I can help them achieve those goals.

I recognize that all good, positive, faithful, hopeful, charitable thoughts are inspired of God and that all negative, discouraging, hateful thoughts come from the adversary. I encourage and nurture the positive in myself and others and discourage in myself and others the negative by replacing it with the positive. I actively support and encourage faith, hope, and charity. I have a positive mental attitude.

I am curious and fascinated with life—a kid at heart. I play, joke, tease, love life and its challenges and humor. I am successful in the truest sense of the word. I focus on living life to its fullest, savoring every experience. I am sensual. I stop to see, taste, feel, smell, and listen to the world around me. I am an adventurer. I jump in with both feet and get involved. Sometimes I choose to just sit back and observe, savor, enjoy and be fascinated with life and my experience of it. I value and love my sense of humor and playfulness, my enthusiasm and zest for life and all its experiences. I realize that I am at my best when I am happy, having fun, and making a game of what I am doing. I make sure I'm not too damn serious and I don't sweat the small stuff.

I am a leader who seeks to be as wise as a serpent but harmless as a dove. I take initiative and responsibility for being successful and leading others. I lead, teach, and show others how to be successful by (1) giving others a detailed vision of what the success will look like when we get there; (2) outlining goals based upon our vision; (3) establishing motives by asking "why" we want a certain thing; and (4) outlining a detailed plan of how to accomplish our goals. I present this rough draft of our visions, goals, motives, and plans to the group and refine our program, enlist their support, and receive feedback.

Each day I do the things that put me in control of my thoughts and actions. If thoughts enter my mind that would otherwise detract from my purpose, I immediately begin to recite the song "Amazing Grace," which reminds me of my need to be worthy of inspiration from God in Heaven. As I go throughout my day I am confident because I know that I am doing the things that I have planned to do. I am flexible enough to adapt, as circumstances require changes in my plans.

I am aware of my divine origin, and I always strive for improved communication with my God by having a running dialogue in my mind, thanking him when things go well, and asking advice on what to do next. I think of Him during the day and ask His advice constantly as I make decisions. I am eager each night to share my day with God, and I always begin each day by thanking Him for his blessings and pleading for His constant companionship.

Sunday is a special day for me. I wake up with the determination to be especially patient with my children and to set an example of Christian living for them.

I am excited about my LifeCreed; I know that by listening each day and incorporating these principles into action, I am constantly improving myself.

I feel each day that I am better than the day before and I am excited at my progress. I love to feel the joy that comes from living in total harmony with my beliefs.

Middle-Aged Father with Older Children

My role in life is to perfect myself. This entails daily personal growth through acting more Christ-like each day. The most valued of all experiences are those involving giving and receiving love. By this I mean the development of a closer relationship with my wife and each of my sons and daughters. I exemplify Christ's attitudes and actions in every involvement that I have with them. These actions bring me closer to my Heavenly Father and influence my wife and children to seek that same end.

I serve the Lord as husband and father. I am a close personal friend to my wife. By this I mean that I affirm her in all she does through active listening and by valuing the things that are important to her. I create an atmosphere that encourages my sweetheart to succeed in the things she desires. I am a great confidant because I listen to her thoughts and feelings without rebuff or defensiveness.

I grow closer to my Lord through scripture study each day at 6:30 A.M., searching for what He would have me know and do to serve Him better. I love discussing my life with Him every night and morning, and I listen carefully to His promptings and instructions to increase our relationship to a deeper and more meaningful level. Through scripture study, meditation, and prayer I learn about the lives of great men and find examples of exemplary love. God has blessed me with a reasonable mind and a pleasing personality which help me to give love. I focus on Betty each Friday, Timmy on Monday, Robert each Tuesday, Marci each Wednesday, Sandi on Thursday, and Erin on Saturday. On their special day I mention to each one the joy I feel as I review their unique gifts and talents. I set aside twenty minutes on their special day, creating an environment of love and acceptance. I focus on my deep feelings of love for them and express my gratitude and thankfulness that they are part of my family. I always take Betty out each Friday night on a date to court her. I schedule time for a monthly daddy/daughter, father/son date with each of my children on the twelve-month calendar. These dates are unique and memorable as my no-limit attitude encourages their sharing of dreams and aspirations with me.

I love my own mother and father. I feel great strength and joy in my family association as I have forgiven them of all the real or imagined injustices of my younger years. I view my parents and grandparents, as well as my children and their future children, as part of an unbroken line of God's children who are privileged to associate closely in earth's school.

I am a sensitive person who wants to understand the feelings behind what people say to me. I am an active listener, listening for five minutes before I speak. I then respond to the emotion as well as the words. I question the speaker until I understand both. I am up front and positively assertive, demonstrating my personal regard for everyone with whom I speak.

I have great friendships in my life because I value friends highly and seek constantly to find ways to serve them. By this I mean that I consciously and subconsciously seek and follow up on things that I can do to show others that they are valuable and worthy persons.

I help each of my children to understand and value close friendships and help each to interact in a positive way with people their own age- and, in fact, with people of all ages—through active listening. I am a great example for my children to pattern their lives after as a friend.

I look for the good in everyone I meet and allow all people their weaknesses. I am, therefore, a "safe haven" to those around me as I am able to see and express their strengths through compliments and sincere praise as an automatic and entirely natural act on my part. This draws people to me and helps them to be their best selves.

I am a man of action. By this I mean I get things done and follow good ideas to their completion. I am also thoughtful and wise and consider all possibilities of each issue before committing to a course of action.

I am self-disciplined. I focus my mental powers and creativity and analytically examine all aspects of each challenge and decision that I am blessed to encounter. The tougher the challenge, the more focused I am. My confidence in my own ability and my faith in God's help enable me to be comfortable with upcoming decisions without worry or fear because I relate all decisions to my Creed. I know I always make the best choices because I have all the information that I need.

I value spiritual moments of meditation and prayer, remembering with fondness and awe the deep feeling of peace beyond words which filled my soul when the Lord gave me the spiritual confirmation of my decision to move to this town.

I remember the spiritual experiences I felt up on Weaver Mountain, in Madison and Rock Canyons, and at Yellowstone Lake.

I enjoy the weekly opportunity to share my special experiences with my family and to plan our lives together in family council. I encourage all the family to attend this important meeting; we always schedule it in our planning meeting on the first Sunday of each month at 4:30 P.M.

I am absolutely delighted with our new home and now have it completely furnished. Betty is really proud of it and loves showing it to our family and friends. I put her first in my life and have rewarded her for her strong support and help for the last 28 years. She no longer feels like she has to "make do" and hope for better times. I feel like I have provided her with a home and lifestyle that she deserves. I appreciate her making our home more attractive and enjoyable and always tell her so.

The atmosphere in my home is constantly improving because I compliment and positively affirm my loved ones continually. Because I am happy with myself, I am happy with those around me. I am easy to get along with, tolerant and pleasant. As I return from work each day I put my business cares aside and think about how much my wife and children need my strength and good attitude. I find something specific to compliment my wife on and do all I can to create an atmosphere in which she can grow and bloom into the choice woman she wants to be. I include her in my life, both business and personal. I talk with her and seek her advice. I trust her, feel close to her, and am strengthened by her. I constantly search for ways to show her affection. I let her know my feelings and I am sensitive to her feelings. I enjoy giving her the things she desires. She is unique and important to me and I express this to her every day. I help with the housework and look for ways to lighten her load. I compliment her on her appearance and keep myself in shape to inspire her to stay in shape. I am her friend and confidant, someone she can lean on, trust, and depend on for support. I laugh with her and enjoy sharing those little humorous anecdotes that happen every day. Nothing comes before my wife.

I investigate and broadcast the successes of each family member. We celebrate those victories and revel in the unique strengths of each other. When adversity or defeat comes, I am supportive, strong, and understanding. I respond to their feelings because I respond to my own feelings. I acknowledge the validity of the other person's feelings without judgment or denial.

Our most relaxed times at home come during quiet evenings when we warm ourselves before the fire in the fireplace. There is time then for one-on-one interaction which I actively seek.

Our favorite winter family activity is skiing. I enjoy those excursions together into the mountains where we can appreciate the fabulous beauty of the winter landscape. I find great happiness in seeing my family enjoy the interaction and the activity, as well as the beauty. We ski together eight days each season and schedule these in our yearly planner so they are not neglected. We similarly enjoy water skiing in the summer for many of the same reasons and schedule eight days annually in our family planner.

Each day I move closer to my perfect physical body, one with tremendous endurance and stamina. Because of my strict exercise program and diet, I possess amazing reserves of energy and have the capacity to accomplish tremendous work at a high level of activity. As I visualize my ideal body, I have very powerful leg and back muscles and a flat stomach. My upper body is well muscled and firm. I weigh 177 pounds and I am a hunk.

Aerobic exercise keeps my body in good shape and gives me a feeling of well-being. I always start my day at 6:00 A.M. with 20 minutes of exercise on the Nordic track at a heart rate of 145; then I do 10 minutes of strength-building exercise.

I render community service through my church and as a parent who is actively involved in the affairs of the schools. I always attend parent-teacher conferences and go prepared to discuss specific issues of concern to me and to my children. Each teacher knows who I am. I always share my deep concern for quality education for each of my children.

I am so grateful for this wonderful life I have. Life is really beautiful.

Putting it All Together for Women

Young Working Mother—Married

I am Dr. Ann Doe and I have a wonderful life. I am the one who determines what I do each day and I am the only one who determines how I react to the people and the situations around me. Therefore, I am happy because I choose to be happy. I listen to this magnificent Creed at least three times every day because it keeps me focused on the wonderful goals and priorities I have set for myself.

I am well organized because I have the greatest daily schedule. It really helps me keep my life in order! Each morning at 6:30 A.M. I jump from my bed filled with enthusiasm for a new day. I love my special exercise time from 6:45 to 7:15 A.M. It really invigorates me physically and it makes me feel so great about my gorgeous body! I love taking care of myself and I always look fantastic and well put together. My elegant, classic wardrobe is such a delight to wear. I really enjoy acquiring one new coordinate to add to it each month. I take care of myself so that my husband's eyes constantly reflect the pride he feels in having such a great-looking wife. I set aside time each morning from 8:00 to 9:00 to keep our beautiful, large custom-built home neat and clean.

I love my family more than anything else in this world and I love being a great example to them. I have an aura about me that draws my husband and children to me. It says to them, "You are important to me. I love you. I support you. I actively listen to what you are thinking and saying. How do you feel? What can I do to make life better for you?"

I am a fantastic companion to my husband. I am constantly aware of his needs and I create circumstances where great communication takes place between us. My husband knows he is first in my life because of the way I treat him in word and action. I look forward to our weekly date night because it gives me another chance to be together with my best friend. We especially enjoy going out to eat and attending concerts together. As part of our special night, I always ask Richard how I can be a better wife, companion for him, and mother to our children. I put his suggestions in this life creed.

Richard and I love to travel. We spend one month each year traveling. We especially enjoy traveling around our beautiful country, but we also consider ourselves to be citizens of the world. I am anxiously anticipating our exciting trips to Europe, Canada, New Zealand, and the South Sea Islands that are coming up as scheduled in our ten-year planner.

I love each one of my five beautiful children. I treasure the time I spend with them! I like my children as people and I enjoy talking to them. I go to all their activities and I support them with my presence and with my enthusiasm. I am absolutely committed to keeping a scrapbook for each of my children. To that end I set aside the first Friday morning of each month to work on these special records.

I am committed to taking one formal class each school year to feed my curiosity about the world around me. I discover one new thing about the world each day and I pass along those insights to my children every day as I help them with their homework from 7:00 to 7:30 P.M. I am also a voracious reader and spend twenty minutes every evening at 9:00 P.M. reading a good book.

I am so very thankful for the gifts of an understanding heart, compassion, and intelligence that I have been blessed with. I relish the opportunity I have each Sunday from 4:00 to 5:00 P.M. to reflect on the things I am doing well, to set new goals for myself, and to prepare myself for the things that are going to happen in the coming weeks and months. I am absolutely committed to keeping a journal of my life for me and for my children. I write in it every Sunday night during my reflection time.

Family Council on Sunday night is sacred in our home. I carefully prepare each week so that I am ready to support and participate in this choice family activity. I am committed to making birthdays and holidays around our house something special. I actively work to find and implement or develop new traditions that help us enjoy these times together even more.

I treasure the opportunity I have to attend church each week with my family. I am always prepared to partake of the Spirit that is there and I learn something new about our Lord every time I go to church.

273

I love taking my family to church with me. I am so excited about it that I am able to motivate them to leave early enough so that we can be in our seats 5 minutes before church starts.

I have been blessed with so many wonderful things: I am healthy and strong, I have a Heavenly Father who loves me, a family that idolizes me, and a husband who thinks the world revolves around me because I work so hard at deserving these blessings. Because I know there are many who do not have these same blessings, I reach out to them through the service I perform for my community. I spend several hours each month helping those who are less fortunate than I am. My favorite charities are public radio and TV, the Red Cross, and shelters for abused women and children. It's so nice to be able to share my financial resources, as well as my time, with these great causes.

People are awed by my ability to remember their names. I am a great listener and I always find out what the other person is thinking before I speak. People come to me with their problems because they can tell by my actions and attitudes that I am a person who really cares about them.

I enjoy the professional work that I do. My work place is a fantastic, interesting, and intellectually stimulating place. There are so many exciting, financially viable projects being developed by our company! I know I make a valuable contribution to this company with my honed organizational skills.

My motto is "Do it now." I always do what I commit to and I make every deadline. I am always honest and straightforward in my dealings with my colleagues and I communicate with them openly and truthfully at all times.

I finish my PhD in October two years from now, and I stay up to date in my field by reading professional magazines and journals from 4:30 to 5:00 P.M. every weekday. I love my part-time job teaching undergraduate and graduate students at the university and am so grateful to have the greatest research project imaginable.

All in all, I think I have a wonderful life and I wouldn't trade places with anyone in the world!

Working Mother—Single

I am so happy to be alive. I love my life and the opportunities that I have for growth and success.

I am organized. I am always on time to every appointment. I arise at 6:00 A.M. every morning, pray, and write in my journal. I awake excited for another day and I feel great because I always get the needed rest for my body and mind. During the weekdays I always go to bed at 11:00 P.M.

Because my life is organized I have plenty of time for all areas of my life: social, mental, physical, spiritual, and family. I am creative and very successful at earning a living. I am financially secure. I always have ideas for creating an income for myself and my family.

In January six years from now, my income is $100,000 per year. I have $50,000 in a life's savings account. I am in total control of my spending and live by a budget. I have a comfortable life as my needs for clothing, food, and shelter, are always met. I am able to travel to Europe once a year, and I always pay cash. I have no debt. I am free to completely enjoy the challenge of free enterprise.

I am admired and respected by my family and peers. My brothers often ask for my opinion and advice on financial matters, and I have been able to lend them money on occasion at an interest rate below the bank's current lending rate. When they speak to me, the look in their eyes and the tone of their voices communicate admiration and respect, and even a bit of reverence. They are appreciative of my help because I give good, sound financial advice.

I love my work. I am excited to see each client. I have the highest regard for every person. They are unique and I am always happy to have the opportunity to use my talents. My creative juices really flow in my workplace. I have endless ideas and inspiration. My workspace is always clean and organized. I love being there because I always have the necessary tools and supplies to do whatever my client's desire.

I often travel to shows and classes. I attend a week long seminar at least once a year. Because I do well and am financially secure, I am able to pay for travel expenses and maintain my home and business while I am away.

My expertise in my field is sought after by my peers because I am well versed in the latest methods of (my business). I am grateful for my talents, always excited to improve them and share my knowledge and skills with others.

I always finish what I start. Whatever project I start gets completed with the same enthusiasm and integrity that it was started. I complete art projects, home improvements, business, and family commitments. I always keep my word to friends, family, and business associates, and especially to myself. I am reliable and constant.

I only commit to those projects I know I can finish and I do quality work. I give my best effort. I have a tremendous amount of energy and talent and I am absolutely dependable.

I bike every morning at 7:00 A.M. I ride seven to ten miles per day. I also work out at the spa three times a week on Monday, Wednesday, and Friday from 10:00 to 11:00 A.M. I love to exercise because it makes me feel great. My lung capacity is constantly improving, my body is cleansing itself of toxins, my muscles are getting stronger and tighter. I am feeling better as I grow older. My skin is getting tighter as well and it glows with health and vitality. I have the look of an athlete. I feel the dedication and competitive spirit of an individual who wins. My body is becoming increasingly lean, muscles well defined. When I walk into the gym guys stare. They are both intimidated and admiring. I am a winner. I work hard and I achieve my goals. I push my muscles to the limit. I thank God for my strong, healthy body. I am graceful as well as strong. I am a dancer. I feel rhythm and movement. I am a combination of femininity and strength, of softness and courage.

I am at peace with my body. I treat it with love and respect. I eat only good foods. I eat fruits and vegetables, grains and pasta. I eat smaller amounts of lean meats, fish, and dairy products. I love to drink water-cool, refreshing, wonderful, water. When I drink water I feel it flushing the toxins and fats out of my body. I feel it moisturizing my body, my skin. I drink at least two quarts of water per day. I am young, healthy and happy. I am complete. I am proud of my body and my face. I am gifted in body and mind. I overcome any obstacle. I am alive and aware. I am in control. Life is wonderful!

I am a caring person. I am sensitive and responsive to people's needs. I am expressive and loving. I create great friendships and loyalties because I give great love and loyalty. I am intelligent and sensitive and love a good time. I have the ability to see humor and use my wit to soften life's stressful times. I am resilient and strong.

277

I love to dance and sing. I love adventure and excitement. Life is always a challenge, an opportunity. I always find the bright and hopeful side to a challenge.

I love peace and harmony in my home. I have an excellent relationship with Judy because I actively listen to her. At mealtime we always discuss her day; at bedtime I take time to listen to her prayers, and then I softly scratch her back to relax her. I am sensitive to her feelings. Bedtime is a special time for us to talk and listen to each other and review the day's events.

Judy is a joy to me, an inspiration. I ask Judy how I can be a better mom and I listen. I give wise counsel to my daughter. I have infinite patience. I respond to frustrating situations with calmness and serenity. I express my concerns with love.

I create an atmosphere of love and acceptance in my home. My child and her friends feel unconditional love and freedom to grow and develop their individual, unique gifts and personalities. Because I am nonjudgmental and see the good in individuals, and because I use my sense of humor, my home often rings with laughter, abounding in warmth and love.

I create an atmosphere where Judy is taught and encouraged by example and word to have good manners and consideration for others' feelings. My actions always demand respect. I tolerate only loving and kind behavior. Everyone's space is of equal importance in my home.

I am consistent. I have the strength and ability to accomplish my goals. I am not alone. I need and accept God's help and love, and also the friendship and advice from those persons whose wisdom and experience exceed my own. Because I am intelligent and successful I welcome and appreciate the counsel of positive and successful people.

I seek constant and continual encouragement and give the same. I align myself with the loving, positive, good powers and energies of the universe.

I am good and I respond to love-love of God, love for myself, and love for my fellowman. I am committed to my course.

I choose to do right and worship God in deed and thought. I give thanks for my blessings. I acknowledge the power and the authority of God and His servants. I am in His service and in His debt. I thank Him always, day and night.

Single Woman

I awake and arise at 6:00 A.M., joyful at facing a day full of opportunity. I look forward to beginning the day. I feel rested and alert and excited to see what the day will bring. I exercise for 45 minutes with my heart rate at 132 for 20 minutes. I choose walking, aerobics, or using the ski machine. When I am walking I feel myself in tune with the trees and breeze; my soul renews as I walk. I happily search for opportunities to walk alone or with Sarah. I enjoy the exercise, feeling my muscles stretching, growing taut, relaxing, and my body growing lean and healthy. My body reacts to exercise by increasing circulation, metabolizing food well, ridding itself of toxins, balancing hormones, and using oxygen well. With each exercise session I feel stronger, healthier, and the exercise becomes easier.

I keep a vision of my ideal self in my mind. I stand tall, with good posture, moving gracefully and with poise. I have energy. My body is firm and well-shaped and I have confidence in how I look. My hair and nails are healthy and well groomed. My body is clean and sweet smelling. I am 5 foot 6 inches and weigh 125 pounds. My eye-hand coordination is excellent and I enjoy playing volleyball, tennis, softball,

279

and group sports. I particularly love to dance. My body responds well to the demands made by my mind as it expresses my feelings and responds to the music. I dance jazz, Latin, and ballroom style. I attract partners in partner dancing because I keep myself well practiced in various dances. I delight in body control and my ability to express myself well through dance. I am in harmony with my body and appreciate its added dimension to my soul. I take good care of my body, giving it 12 glasses of water each day, which efficiently serves my body's needs.

I eat grains, fruits, and vegetables. My body accepts the food easily, using it effectively. I enjoy eating and eat until filled. Because I exercise and eat nutritious foods, my body is increasingly efficient at burning excess fat quickly so that I become more lean and trim. Each day my stomach gets flatter, my legs stronger and more slim, my buns tighter, and my back straighter. My body is limber, lively, strong and works well. It never lets me down.

I enjoy feeling the clothes fall on my increasingly lean body and slither down. I have abundant energy because my body is extremely well conditioned and very well maintained. Every day I feel an increase in stamina. To ensure that I enjoy life to its fullest, I take extreme care to eat well prepared, nourishing meals. I plan them ahead, always eating three meals a day. I make sure that I always eat them at a regular time. I savor the flavor of good foods. I make sure that each meal includes several vegetables and grains. I eat slowly and chew carefully. I enjoy the preparation and anticipation of the coming meal.

I obtain power from righteous living. The ever-growing strength in my spirit causes me to eschew evil. I love being a daughter of Heavenly Father; I have a glow and warmth from that love. I open my heart to feel His approval and appreciation. My high self-esteem comes from my relationship with Him and I tenderly protect that relationship. Each morning at 7:15 I have an hour of meditation and planning time right after I have dressed for the day. I read the scriptures and study guides as I seek for greater understanding. I thoughtfully prepare and then speak with the Lord. I respectfully approach Him and carefully listen to His direction and teachings to me. I tune into His strength and power and add to my own. I speak with the Lord honestly and openly. My prayers are purposeful and meaningful. I have confidence that I understand His directions and trust my ability to respond to His promptings.

I am optimistic. I expect the best.

I recognize the value of my time, resources, and energy and wisely make decisions on spending them. I see what steps need to be taken and what resources are needed. I effectively judge the energy required from me and make allocations of my time and resources for that which I want most in life. I master my time so that I handle stress easily. I schedule time carefully and keep the commitments I have made. I choose uplifting and enlightening books, movies, and television pro-grams. I choose to be with people who uplift and enlighten, but learn from everyone I am around. I relax well, even as I go about my daily routine. I am slow to jump to conclusions and calm in a crisis. If I feel stress I recognize it, take time to stretch and rid my body of its effects, close my eyes for a moment, and calm myself.

I am fun to be around—spontaneous, creative, and exciting. I am positive and happy and have an uncanny ability to attract quality people. I enjoy life. That joy is contagious to those around me. I have a rewarding time establishing and maintaining relationships and look forward to spending time with friends, both men and women. People

281

seek to be with me. They sense there are wonderful things in my soul and our bonds grow.

When I meet people I look them in the eyes. I observe good points about each person, mention it when appropriate, and use it to remember that person. I notice their eyes-the color, expression, and physical features around them. I key in on their eyes the next time I see them and it reminds me of their names. I use their names at least three times in the conversation. I have a great memory for names. I always key my memory by saying, "What is that person's name? It will come to me in a minute."

I sense my capacity to remember growing each day. I use this skill to memorize a scripture, quote, or poem each week. The mental exercise is very rewarding. I am so excited to learn that I stay wide-awake and alert while reading. My mind is focused. I study things and people around me. I notice changes in people and I take note of my environment. I read magazines, books, and newspapers. I read religious information, current events, self-improvement topics, the classics, and much more. I particularly enjoy reading on Sunday when I have time to concentrate and relax. I remember what I read with excellent recall.

I easily grasp new concepts and am stimulated when using my brain to understand, memorize, and find solutions.

I am gracious and appreciative. When others are giving or kind I am responsive and grateful. I graciously accept others' giving to me, but judge well before asking too much of anyone. I acknowledge those who have a part of my life and my personality.

I am generous. I constantly surprise people anonymously, receiving great joy from doing so. I am the first to laugh at my own mistakes, trying to help others not to feel self-conscious or ill at ease when they make mistakes.

I make a point of giving honest compliments and praise. I am a good conversationalist. I keep myself well-informed on current events and issues and am able to discuss them intelligently. I have a talent for putting my thoughts into words that express my feelings and ideas. I say what I am thinking and feeling in a concise and interesting way, being diplomatic and tactful. I am honest and real. I tell people how I feel and am true to myself without feeling guilty. I am gentle and kind, but firm when necessary. I recognize when it is important to share from myself. I remember stories and incidents and clean jokes and bring lightness and laughter into conversations. I am entertaining at appropriate times.

I am an active listener. When I am with others, I look them in the eyes. Each person has my undivided attention until other priorities enter in. Then I kindly extricate myself. I invite others to share in such a way that they are comfortable and at ease. They know they can trust me and that I keep confidences.

I give others space to make their own decisions, control their own lives, and encourage them to reach their potential. I am happy to be a sounding board and like the role of cheerleader for their lives. I also allow them to work out their own problems in the way they choose—expressing confidence in their ability to do so. I give others the benefit of the doubt and realize they may have other perspectives. I allow others their weaknesses, focusing instead on their strengths. I expect the best of others but accept what they give. I am appropriately con-frontive. If I feel tension in a relationship, I work for resolution so the lines of affection are kept open. I seek feedback from those I respect and avoid being defensive. I am aware of actions that make others feel uncomfortable and clearly evaluate the necessity of those actions in my happiness. When someone offends me I deal with the emotions at. that time with the person from whom I took offense.

I feel each day that I am better than the day before, and I am excited at my progress. I love to feel the joy that comes in living in total harmony with my beliefs.

I sing well. My voice is clear and full. It's easy to breathe correctly. My diaphragm moves properly to support the tone and I easily reach notes in a broad range.

I like learning new ideas. I like deep thinking and problem solving. I am creative in my thinking. I am good at brainstorming and finding options and possibilities. I have vision and good imagination.

I tole paint with confidence and decisiveness. I visualize the final project, quickly and decisively painting each item, and finding great pleasure in my talent. I also arrange flowers beautifully and finish all crafts well. Whatever I put my hand to I complete, and I learn in the process. I challenge myself and enjoy stretching my abilities.

I am comfortable before a crowd. I enjoy singing, dancing, delivering a speech, or teaching a class. I always prepare very well and have confidence because I am ready.

I love working with youth. I enjoy being their cheerleader and aiding in their search for their souls and personalities. I savor their growth and point out their strengths. I teach them by example and personal contact. I spend time with them, listen to them, and encourage them. When we are together their souls are warmed and they are inspired to believe in themselves.

I thoroughly enjoy my work. I love my clients. When clients meet me, they feel that they can trust me and that I have a great deal of knowledge about my field. They sense respect and warmth from me. I have great insight and understanding of those I meet. I am cordial when clients come in and think empathetically about their needs and feelings. Our relationship is always a positive experience for them. I explain well the information I give and they feel that they can ask questions. I am patient with their need for information and reassurance. They feel comfortable with me. I keep in mind the importance of customer satisfaction. I am wise when deciding which clients to take on and which ones will tax our resources too much. On their return visits to the office, I call them by name, often touch them on the shoulder, and acknowledge their importance to our office.

I arrive at the office at 8:30 A.M. The first hour is spent in studying, filing, and preparing for the day. At 9:30 I focus on the files that need my attention the most. I organize my priorities well and stay focused as the other demands of the day present themselves. I use my time effectively, choosing each hour the most effective and important things to do. I approach my clientele with positive expectations. I am com mitted to excellence in my career, always mindful that my personal life comes before the demands of work. I quickly return phone calls and always follow through on assignments that I take on. Deadlines are always met because I plan so well ahead. I wrap up my paperwork by 5:00 P.M. I work hard to be a positive part of our team. I work on ideas until we come together on our desires and are not competing with each other.

I enjoy the office staff. I watch closely for their accomplishments and compliment them specifically. I enlist their help in establishing office rules and expect them to conduct themselves accordingly. They appreciate my leadership and follow easily. We have fun and laughter in the office at appropriate times. They know from my actions and attitude that their happiness is a priority to me. I have an efficient office system and strive to continually improve to meet our clients' needs. I am open to ideas from the staff and enlist their suggestions and feedback. Staff members know that they can approach me for counsel, that I am wise and fair in making decisions. I approach them in an open, easy, happy, grateful manner. I am generous with praise. I pitch in whenever necessary to take action in resolving conflicts and problems. I speak well of them to others. I am favorably viewed by upper management and, when I am with them, I converse easily.

I have a keen sense for recognizing honest and profitable business ideas. In four years my earnings are $85,000; in six years my earnings are $100,000; and in eight years my earnings are $120,000. I save ten percent of my income and keep a savings account of $25,000 for emergencies for myself or my family. I seldom use credit, using cash for most purchases. I am mastering the discipline of budgeting. I use the utmost prudence and sensibility when spending money. I save $40.00 monthly for "The Sisters" reunion. In one year we are flying to Boston for a vacation. My savings allows us to schedule other vacations together every other year. I enjoy our home and furnishings and the wardrobe that my income produces. I receive satisfaction and joy by performing anonymous acts of giving to those in need. My income allows me to send money, flowers, gift certificates, or food when I recognize a way I can help.

Giving of my time and efforts is always more important than money. I am descriptively precise in writing my Creed. I listen to it daily and my subconscious mind recommits to the values and expectations I have for myself. On the first Sunday of each month I review my goals and my Creed and make changes as warranted. I anticipate these reviews and enjoy the growth and planning. I record my feelings in my journal daily, especially noting spiritual insight, growth, under-standing, and accomplishments.

My strong, well-directed inner drive and brilliant imagination allow me to visualize myself reaching my goals. My mind, heart, and spirit are united and congruent, creating a power and force that gives me all I desire.

Register to Receive Your FREE Acclerated-Learning Music CD

Have you ever noticed how much more powerful a movie is if the soundtrack is really well done? It seems to be a more emotional experience, and everything else about the movie seems more powerful. Think of Accelerated-Learning Music as the soundtrack to your LifeCreed. Music has the ability to jump right to the emotional areas of our mind, and our LifeCreed is carried along.

You will record your LifeCreed with specific accelerated-learning music playing in the background. As reported in Ostrander and Schrader's book *Super Learning*, scientists in the former Soviet Bloc were first to make the startling discovery that a certain kind of music can put the mind-brain into an accelerated-learning state. Since that time, extensive research has clearly shown that the larghetto or andante movements in Baroque concertos, a restful tempo of about 60 beats per minute, actually open up pathways and connections throughout the mind-brain, accelerating the formation and expansion of mental models. Baroque composers typical scored this peaceful, soothing music for string instruments. Accelerated-Learning Music super-charges your LifeCreed and your results.

This Audio CD was prepared by LifeBalance Institute as the perfect soundtrack for your LifeCreed. Complete the form below and mail to us. Your Accelerated-Learning Music CD will be sent to you at no additional cost.

You can also visit us at www.lifebal.net for additional products and information.

Send your completed form to:
LifeBalance Institute
105 South State Street #226
Orem, Utah 84058

Name: _____

Address: _____

City: _____ **State:** _____

Zip Code: _____

Telephone Number (____) _____

Email Address: _____